A BLACK PHYSICIAN'S STORY
Bringing Hope in Mississippi

Douglas L. Conner, M.D.

A
BLACK
PHYSICIAN'S
STORY

Bringing Hope in Mississippi

Douglas L. Conner, M.D.,
with John F. Marszalek
Foreword by Aaron Henry

UNIVERSITY PRESS OF MISSISSIPPI
Jackson

Library of Congress Cataloging in Publication Data

Conner, Douglas L.
  A Black physician's story

  Includes index.
  1. Conner, Douglas L. 2. Afro-American physicians—
Mississippi—Starkville—Biography. I. Marszalek,
John F., 1939–   II. Title
R154.C556A33 1985   610′.92′4 [B]   85-9106
ISBN 0-87805-279-8

The photographs on pages 4 and 16 are reprinted from
Kenneth G. McCarty, ed., *Hattiesburg: A Pictorial
History* (Jackson: University Press of Mississippi, 1982).
The photograph on page 4 is reprinted with the per-
mission of the photographer, Mary Ann Wells. The
photograph on page 24 is reprinted from Melerson Guy
Dunham, *Centennial History of Alcorn A. & M. College*
(Hattiesburg: University and College Press of Missis-
sippi, 1971).

CONTENTS

FOREWORD

The man who is the subject of this book has been a true inspiration to me as well as a friend and associate. I first came to know Dr. Douglas Conner in 1961. I had graduated from the School of Pharmacy at Xavier University and had opened a drugstore in Clarksdale. He had completed his medical training and had set up his office in Starkville. We were both members of the all-black North Mississippi Medical, Dental, and Pharmaceutical Association. The "Society" met in the homes of the membership, which was scattered all over the northern half of Mississippi. During these meetings I came to respect and admire Dr. Conner. By the time I got to know him, I had already had about ten years of involvement with civil rights activities in Mississippi and the nation. Dr. Conner impressed me as a person who believed in the necessity of moving the black community forward—both by pushing and pulling.

Over the years I have come to know Doug Conner well. I have come to see him as a person more concerned with putting people on their own two feet than with putting a man on the moon. Dr. Conner is as much a great teacher as he is a great friend. He is also a great leader, content to have his ideas pressed to fruition by others whose enthusiasm he has kindled. Doug has always emphasized the fact that human progress never rolls in automatically on the wheels of inevitability. He knows it comes through the tireless efforts of men and women willing to be co-workers with God. He knows too that, without this hard work, time itself becomes an ally of the forces of social stagnation. He urges all to use time creatively in the knowledge that the time is always ripe to do right. Now is the time, he has always said, to make the promises of democracy real and transform our pending national elegy into a creative psalm of Brotherhood. He has always said that this is the time to lift our national policy from the quicksand of racial injustice to the solid rock of human dignity.

Dr. Conner subscribes to the philosophy that it is our duty to keep up the agitation for our rights, not only for our sake alone but also for the sake of the nation at large. He knows that it is against our interest not to do so, and that it would be unpatriotic for us to acquiesce in the present, for the present is a wrong condition of things. If justice sleeps in this land, let it not be because we helped lull it to sleep by our silence, our indifference. Let it not be from lack of effort on our part to arouse it from its slumbers. This is Dr. Conner's philosophy, and this is the way he has conducted his life all the years I have known him, whether in the NAACP, the Democratic Party, in the midst of school integration or economic boycotts, or in his treatment of his patients.

In short, what Dr. Conner believes in and has always fought for is that we all do our duty—to our nation, to ourselves, to our children, and to our children's children. Let us then continue to do the basic job of making America America again, this time for everyone!

Aaron Henry

PREFACE

He is a tall slim man, his appearance belying his years. Except for his white hair and some wrinkles in his face, he looks very much as he did when he was a young doctor. His schedule has not changed much either. From the moment he rises early in the morning to make his hospital visits or assist in surgery or deliver a baby, through his hectic office schedule, to evening and late night civic meetings, he is constantly in motion. No matter where he is, the telephone constantly rings for him. Patients, doctors, and nurses looking for medical advice, and individuals seeking all kinds of non-medical aid are constantly consulting him. Civic leaders ask him to take on yet another committee or attend another important meeting. Throughout all this activity, he remains placid. All his life he has been "bringing hope in Mississippi," and he shows no signs of letting up.

I first met Doug Conner sometime after I arrived in Starkville to join the History faculty of Mississippi State University in the summer of 1973. Since one of my fields of scholarly interest is Afro-American history, I immediately began looking at the Starkville community from that perspective. Doug Conner's name cropped up everywhere I looked. I heard of his role in pioneering black political participation in Starkville and of his long and hard efforts to help bring about integration of the schools and greater economic opportunity for blacks in Starkville's business life. I repeatedly read about him in the newspaper commenting on local issues as the city's major black leader. I developed a picture of him as a serious, hard-driving, uncompromising individual.

I first met him at a crowded civic function, and the experience surprised me. He proved to be soft-spoken, exceedingly considerate, with a good sense of humor and an easy laugh. He impressed me as a person of great patience, content within himself, happy with what he had already accomplished but even more aware of what he still needed to do. He did not dominate the conversations that swirled around him nor did he stand out in the gathering. If I had not seen his picture in the paper, I doubt whether I would have realized who he was.

Over the next several years we saw each other at various public gatherings, but we did not establish a close relationship. When I collaborated with Sadye Wier to write an account of her husband's life as the first black businessman on the main street of Starkville, Doug and I came to know each other better. He had been very close to Robert Wier coming to see his wife's uncle as a second father. He was pleased to see Robert Wier's life historically preserved. At the time Sadye told me that someday someone had to preserve Doug's life story too. I agreed, but that was the extent of the discussion.

I can not remember the details of the decision to write Doug's life story. I do know, however, that Sadye Wier was the primary agent in causing it to happen. She brought the two of us together at her home to discuss the project and, as only Sadye can, encouraged us to get on with it.

This book is the result of this collaboration: Doug's memories and papers, public records, Sadye's scrapbooks of newspaper accounts and pictures, and my ability to draw together all the information. This is Doug's book, the story of his life and activities as seen through his eyes and expressed in his quiet, unassuming style. Gathering the information and writing the book was a slow process because of Doug's many responsibilities and my teaching and research commitments. Whenever we could, however, we would meet in Sadye's dining room and fortified with the home-made cake she always provided, conduct an extended interview on some aspect of Doug's life. He dealt with every topic in the matter-of-fact manner I came to see was his personality. Often he seemed mystified when I commented on the importance of this or that aspect of his life. "It was nothing," he would say, insisting that he had done nothing more than anyone else would have done under the same circumstances. Other times, he would worry: "Are you sure I'm not doing too much bragging?" "No," I would reply, "You're just presenting the facts, so future generations of Mississippians will know what was going on during these years." "O.K., then," he would say with relief. "I don't want this book to be any kind of memorial. What I want is a book that will show blacks and whites who read it that a black person can make it if he or she works at it. Other people inspired me to strive to do my best. I want this book to do the same for others, particularly young people."

As I listened to Doug make variations of this same comment throughout our many hours of interviews and tapings, I thought about what he was saying. I could see what he meant, and I partially agreed with him. As a historian, however, I was more concerned with accurately preserving an essential aspect of the past. I would be pleased if the book proved to be an inspiration, but I wanted it, above all else, to be a document of black life and an insight into what it meant to be black in Mississippi during the dark days of segregation and into the promising days of integration.

Many people played important roles in the publication of this book. At Mississippi State University, William E. Parrish, Head, and Robert L. Jenkins, Department of History; Edward L. McGlone, Dean, College of Arts and Sciences; Robert E. Wolverton, Vice President for Academic Affairs; James D. McComas, President, were all personally encouraging and supportive of the project. Juanita Conner and Jeanne Marszalek provided love and inspiration. The staff of the United States District Court in Aberdeen Mississippi provided access to necessary court documents. Charles Pearce of the Mississippi Department of Archives and History provided important aid in locating photographs. Seetha Srinivasan and JoAnne Prichard of the University Press of Mississippi steadily guided the manuscript toward publication, and the staff of the Mitchell Memorial Library, Mississippi State University, provided their usual excellent support. Finally, without Sadye Wier's quiet determination, the project might never have begun. Though she is not a professional historian, she understands the importance of preserving the past and has made contributions to Mississippi history from which future generations will benefit.

John F. Marszalek

A BLACK PHYSICIAN'S STORY
Bringing Hope in Mississippi

1
CHILDHOOD

I was born in Hattiesburg, Mississippi, on October 25, 1920, delivered by Miss Goldmine, the local midwife. Until I was twelve I lived on Curry Street in Newman's Quarters, an all-black neighborhood between the J. J. Newman Lumber Company and a railroad track. My father was Jerry Conner, a fireman in the lumberyard; my mother was Mary Elnora Washington Conner, a custodian for the city's telephone exchange.

Although my knowledge of my genealogy is sparse (I cannot trace my family back beyond the late nineteenth century), I know that my paternal grandparents came from Shubuta, a small town near Hattiesburg, and that my paternal grandfather, Elijah Conner, died in Shubuta before I was born. My grandmother, Maggie Conner, moved to Hattiesburg and lived right next to us in a large house at the end of our street. We saw her all the time, but I never knew anything about her past; she was simply "Big Momma" to everyone in the family. (In contrast, my mother was "Little Momma.") Big Momma always wore an apron, and she ruled the entire family with a firm hand. She loved to dip Garrett snuff; we youngsters often had to get her a large bottle from the neighborhood store. We always knew she was out of snuff when she became very hard to deal with! My grandmother was an imposing figure, snuff or no. She played a major part in my early childhood.

My grandfather on my mother's side was Ras Washington. My maternal grandmother had died during childbirth, so I never knew her. My grandfather remarried, and he and his second wife lived in another Hattiesburg black neighborhood about five or six miles away from us. Our family would often walk to see them, and it was always a treat. They owned cows, and there was always fresh milk and buttermilk to drink and good country butter to eat. My grandmother loved to cook, and I remember how good the food always was. Sometimes we would spend weekends there, being spoiled by these typically indulgent grandparents.

My most glamourous relative was no doubt one of my maternal great-grandfathers. I only saw him once, but it was a sight I have never forgotten. I was not even ten years old when I saw standing before me one day at my grandfather's this full-blooded Choctaw Indian in full regalia. I was awestruck. It was a mark of real distinction to me as a child to know that I was part Indian, and I was amazed that none of my adult relatives seemed equally awed.

I know very little about my parents' backgrounds. My father was born in Shubuta in 1898, and my mother in Hinds County in 1900. They were married in Hattiesburg in 1916 or 1917. My mother told us that she married young because she did not get along with her stepmother and wanted her independence. Yet, when my parents were first married, they moved in with my paternal grandmother. Since Big Momma had had ten children and some of them were already gone, her house was large enough for her to be able to take in my parents. As soon as we children came along, however, my parents built their own house next door to Big Momma's.

There were four children in our family. My sister Corrine was born first in 1918; then I came along in 1920. Two years later my brother Earnest was born, and in 1932 my brother William. Of these four children, three lived into late adulthood and all lived successful lives, except for Earnest, who was always rowdy and in trouble. Earnest was killed in a fight during a gambling game in Picayune when he was in his early twenties.

The neighborhood where we lived, Newman's Quarters, got its name from the J. J. Newman Lumber Company, a major employer of Hattiesburg blacks during the 1920s. The company built several rows of shotgun houses straddling the railroad siding leading into the lumberyard from the Illinois Central main line. The neighborhood consisted of three unpaved streets with well-kept houses and yards along both sides of them. Our house was about two hundred yards from the railroad tracks and a quarter of a mile from the lumber-yard.

The neighborhood had a neat appearance about it. My mother was always after us to keep our yard clean, and we spent a lot of time sweeping and cleaning. Across the street from us lived a lady whose yard was the neighborhood's garden spot. I can remember watching the many butterflies flitting among the foliage on her property. People would often come to this yard to get bouquets of flowers to brighten up their homes. Since practically everyone in the neighborhood worked for the lumberyard, we developed a real closeness. In case of sickness or trouble of any kind, the neighbors could be depended upon to rally around.

The neighborhood's major problem was its location on low ground. Every year, when the Leaf River rose, that section of the town flooded, the water rising to five inches or so above our house's floor level. When this happened,

Hattiesburg Depot: near here a young Douglas Conner early experienced the effects of segregation.

we packed up our things and moved in with my grand-parents on the other side of town until the flood waters receded.

Our house stood out in this neighborhood of fifty to sixty houses because it (like my grandmother's) was larger than the neighbors' shotgun houses. My father built it when we children came along. It was made of wood, had a kitchen, a living room, and two bedrooms. It was hardly elaborate, but it was comfortable. In addition, there was an outhouse (which was a real adventure to visit at night during the dead of winter!), a small smokehouse, and small pens for several pigs. Chickens had the run of the property, which was about two hundred feet by two hundred feet in area and which once had held two shotgun houses. There was also a garden where my mother grew such vegetables as corn, beans, and squash. Tomato plants grew in the flower beds next to the house.

Though a few other neighbors bought their shotgun houses and either added to them or tore them down to build new houses, most people in Newman's Quarters lived in company-provided houses. Among poverty-stricken people, then, my family had things a little bit better than some of the rest. My father's and mother's jobs were steady. He worked twelve hours a day, six days a week, and my mother's job as cleaning lady at the telephone exchange was considered favored employment for a black woman.

We always had enough to eat, though there were times such as Sunday dinner when we wished for more. This meal was never considered complete unless we ate one of the chickens my mother raised in our yard. We always hoped she would not invite our minister to dinner on Sunday or that our relatives would not come by for a visit. If either of these things happened, we children would end up eating the neck or the wings while our company ate the preferred pieces. If too many people came at once, we would eat more dressing then chicken, wishing under our breath for the finer parts our visitors were consuming at our expense.

Most of our meals centered around pork. We always had at least one hog in the backyard pen. In the fall at the proper time the neighbors would conduct a kill in which our family participated. The slaughtered hog or hogs would be salted and smoked for use during the following year. On weekdays we usually had only two meals: breakfast in the morning and supper in the evening. Lunch—we called it dinner then—was a hit-and-miss affair most of the time. Breakfast was a major meal—fatback, grits, eggs, and my mother's biscuits. I can still remember how good those biscuits were! Our evening meal usually consisted of a lot of vegetables and a little pork.

I can also remember times when we had only bread and water to eat. My mother had a rule, though: we had to eat what the family provided and be satisfied. No matter how little or how much we had to eat, we were never allowed to take any food from anyone else. Even if we were hungry when we went to visit someone and were offered something to eat, even sweets, my mother insisted that we say, "No thank you, I'm full." Heaven help us if we did not comply with this mandate!

From my earliest days I can remember spending a lot of my time working. My father's job as fireman consisted of throwing sawdust into a furnace to provide steam power for the yard. It was hard, dirty work, particularly tiring in the heat and humidity of the summer. From the age of six or seven I helped my father during vacation periods from school. At home I also had the job of tending the garden, the hogs, and the chickens. I cut grass in our yard and for neighbors. On wash day I had to get the wood for the fire used to boil the wash water, and I was responsible for filling the wash cauldron and the two rinsing pots. This too was hard work for a child under twelve, but I never minded it that much because I also had time to play games, read, and go to school.

Most of the games I remember playing were the kind that my friends Tommy Hall, Billy McBride, and I made up. The only toys we had we made ourselves. Our family could not afford many, and my mother would not allow us to accept gifts. I particularly remember being fond of making kites. Tommy Hall was good at kite making, and the rest of us would follow his lead. We would go to the nearby woods to get dry straws which we would join with paper and glue and string to construct a kite. We would then fly our home-made kite for hours at a time. We also caught June bugs for bait and went fishing in a nearby stream. Sometimes we constructed makeshift horses out of sticks and pretended we were horseback riders. At other times we would play tag. More often than not, however, I would read rather than play games. Mostly I read adventure stories, magazines, or comic books. My mother and an aunt got books from people for me, and my mother also brought home magazines from the telephone exchange. I never bought books except for a comic once in a while.

I started school when I was seven years old, entering the "primary grade" and then proceeding to the first grade. Later I passed two grades in one year. From grades 1 through 5, I attended East Jerusalem Elementary School, one of three black elementary schools in Hattiesburg at the time. This school was located in the East Jerusalem section of the city, a mile or two from my house. Each morning and every afternoon the children from my neighborhood walked the distance to and from school, passing on the way a brick white school which, of course, was closed to us.

Our school was an old wooden building with a potbel-

7

lied stove in each room. Everything from the desks to the books was a hand-me-down from one of the white elementary schools in town. There were five grades, but there were only four teachers plus the principal. One of the teachers taught two grades at the same time. All the teachers were very devoted to their work and spent long hours with students during and after classes.

I was an average student. I had no real difficulties with my work, though I was not very keen on arithmetic. My favorite school activity was listening to one of the teachers playing the piano. I never studied music myself, but I liked hearing the music played during school programs.

In addition to work, chores, and school, church played an important part in my early childhood. My family belonged to the East Jerusalem Baptist Church, and each Sunday we children would put on our best clothes and walk the several miles to attend Sunday school and the service which immediately followed. My mother usualy went with us, but my father was not a churchgoer. The church's minister was the Reverend Riley Thomas, a dynamic Baptist preacher whose spellbinding manner made him a favorite of his congregation of several hundred people. Our church services were not the highly emotional meetings often associated with southern black congregations. Reverend Thomas was a very intelligent man, and his sermons were heavy on message and light on emotion. Once in a while there would be a little whooping, particularly when a gospel quartet was singing, but most of the time the congregation was restrained.

My church was much different from the Holiness Church which was located near our home in Newman's Quarters. My friends and I would sometimes peek in during one of their services and would be wide-eyed at what we saw. The people in the congregation were Holy Rollers; they rolled on the floor, jumped up and down,

moaned, and screamed. We were mesmerized at the go-
ings on, so different were they from the services we were
used to at our church.

Most of the time, my life as a child had an agreeable
rhythm to it. On school days at around 8 A.M., when my
father was returning from his job at the lumber mill, we
children were leaving for school and my mother was leaving for her work. We ate a large breakfast, my father
sometimes joining us and other times going straight to
bed. My mother worked until about two or three, so she
was home when we returned from school between three
and four. When she was late, my grandmother was next
door, and my father was home because he did not leave for
work until 7 or 8 P.M. After school we did our chores, ate
supper, played, and then went to bed. My mother always
insisted that no matter where we went or what we were
doing, whether on a school/work night or on a Sunday,
we had to be in bed by nine o'clock so we could all get a
good night's rest.

The only holidays we celebrated were Christmas and
the Fourth of July. At Christmas, the relatives would pour
in, and we children had to sleep on the floor while the
visitors took our beds. If the visitors stayed too long, we
awaited their departure anxiously so that we could reclaim
our beds. On the Fourth of July, fireworks were shot off
everywhere around us. Birthdays were not particularly
important days in our lives, but sometimes my mother
would bake a cake and invite in a few neighbors. We celebrated no special black holidays, neither Emancipation
Day on January 1 as blacks used to do in the nineteenth
century nor May 8 as some blacks in other parts of Mississippi still do today. We just never thought in terms of a
holiday to celebrate a black person or a black-related
event. We did not know of any to celebrate.

As I think back on my childhood now, I usually remember the good things, the happy times that made my life pleasant, but I also had experiences that were not so happy. One of the most immediate sadnesses was the fact that my father was an alcoholic. I don't believe I ever saw him completely sober a day of his life. He would be sober enough to go to work and do his job, but during off-duty hours, except when he was sleeping, he was constantly drinking. He was the kind of drinker who withdrew when he drank, and as a result I had very little relationship with him. We rarely talked to one another, not because he was angry with me or I with him but simply because his alcoholism put up a barrier between us. In my early years I didn't think much about it, but as I grew older and wanted to have a closer relationship, it bothered me more and more. I wondered why my father drank. I developed a real hostility toward him. As I went along further in school, I realized that he was trying to get away from some problem. Rack my brain as I might, however, I never discovered exactly what that problem was. He was already drinking before his marriage, and my mother's efforts to change him failed. He drank steadily all their years together. He never said why, and neither did my mother. My father's drinking was a painful fact of my childhood, and it took me a long time to be able to deal with it.

Although I have no way of knowing, I believe my father's alcoholism was responsible for another personal trauma in my life: my father's and mother's divorce. When I was twelve years old, my parents separated permanently and we children had to decide which parent to stay with. We wished the divorce could be avoided, but this was not to be. We had to make a choice. I chose my mother because I had a better relationship with her than with my father. My sister and brother stayed with my father. My mother was pregnant when my parents separated, and my other brother, William, was born just one month later.

My father stayed in our house, and my mother and I moved in with one of her sisters in Aldridge Quarters, about two miles away. We lived there for something like a year. Then another of my mother's sisters asked her to move in with her in another area of town. When this sister married, my mother decided to move to the town of Picayune, where she remarried. I did not want to disrupt my schooling so I stayed in Hattiesburg, moving in with another of my mother's sisters and her husband—Tom and Lillian Patterson. During all these moves I saw my father, Big Momma, my sister, and brother regularly, in addition to having even fuller contact with my mother's family. I also saw firsthand the effects of divorce. Both sides talked to me against the other. It was all very sad.

A major reason for my ability to survive the trauma of divorce was the goodness and generosity of my aunt and uncle. They added me to their family (they had three daughters of their own), and I remained with them until I graduated from high school in 1939, although I did spend one summer with my mother and her new husband. Uncle Tom was the closest thing to a father I ever had until I met Uncle Rob Wier after I was married. Uncle Tom worked in a mattress factory, and was a good, decent, hardworking man. He often took me places with him, talked to me, and showed a real interest in my well-being. I have often wondered what might have happened to me had he and Aunt Lillian not taken me in. My life with them was very similar to my life at home except for the addition of an adult male I could respect and talk to. Still, the divorce left its mark on my life.

An even more potentially destructive element in my childhood was the segregation system under which I grew up. In Hattiesburg, as in all Mississippi towns of that period, segregation was a fact of life. There was a white Hattiesburg and a black Hattiesburg. The two were totally separate. They touched on one another constantly, but they never merged. To be white meant being a part of the power structure; to be black meant being powerless. It meant discrimination at every turn, from inferior schools to no voting rights, to balconies in movie theatres and basement wards in the hospital. Being black meant a life of subordination, a life of limited goals and expectations.

Segregation was so pervasive and so ingrained that it simply existed; it did not have to be studiously applied each day because it was always there, always applied. Whites knew it; blacks knew it even better. That was the way it was, that was the way everyone insisted it had always been and would always be in the future.

Besides being a community factor, segregation was also a personal matter. Each person experienced and reacted to it in his or her own way. Reflecting on my childhood today, I find it difficult to remember specific incidents of discrimination in a life that was encircled by ring upon ring of prejudice. I remember walking to school and passing the white school on the way. I remember white children often waiting for us to taunt us and to engage us in fights. The harassment was even more bitter because of having to pass the white school to get to our black one. I also remember walking in other white areas in town and hearing yells of "Nigger this" and "Nigger that." I remember having to sit in the balcony at the movies, though I enjoyed the western films so much that I ignored the Jim Crow seating and the fact that the Indians always lost out. I was too young to identify my Indian grandfather with the red men I saw on the screen. Day after day I lived with segregation. It was part of my community; it was a part of my life.

No one event alerted me to the meaning of prejudice, but there is one incident that I especially remember. I was very young, probably somewhere between eight and ten years of age. My mother and I were walking into town, and I remember having my best clothes on. It had just rained, and the unpaved street near the railroad station was a sea of mud. We were walking along the sidewalk which, though wet, was clear of mud. Just ahead of us, I remember seeing a white boy about my age walking in our direction. As he drew nearer, my mother suddenly pulled me off the sidewalk and into the mud so the white boy could pass. My fancy clothes and shoes became covered with mud. She said nothing; I said nothing. In my mind, though, I wondered what was so special about this boy that my own mother would pull me into the mud so he could pass by. Even at that age I knew the answer, and it gnawed at me.

I would also become upset when I listened to my parents and relatives discuss politics and their nonrelationship to it. I remember Herbert Hoover and Franklin D. Roosevelt—that is, knowing that Hoover and then Roosevelt was our president—but I don't remember adults talking much about them or about any national events. The Depression did not affect my family directly as my father and mother never lost their jobs. Other blacks I knew suffered severely, and I remember seeing soup lines and other evidences of the economic crisis, but I rarely heard anyone talking about it. No one even talked much about Mississippi's Governor (later Senator) Theodore Bilbo, though as a child I already recognized him as a mean racist. Most of the talk centered on local politics— a mayoral race, the condition of local streets, and other such issues. National politics and national leaders were too distant for any of us to express much interest or thought in them.

I do remember adults bemoaning the fact that they were not permitted to vote and that white folks controlled everything, but no one ever talked of putting the issue to a test. No one dared even think about voting. I don't remember any incidents of violence against blacks; usually it was a matter of blacks fighting blacks. (I particularly remember one of our neighbors shooting another during a gambling argument.) But every now and then there would be a fight between a white person and a black person or several on each side. My mother would always respond the same way: "You're in a white world, and there are certain things you cannot do. You have to be humble."

These attitudes bothered me. My father never said anything, but my mother's resigned attitude, her insistence that it could never be changed, that we blacks had to accept things as they were, was upsetting to me. I remember, even as a young child, asking myself *why* I had to accept things as they were. I never accepted the contention that anyone was better than I was, even though older blacks around me were saying, "You're just a nigger." I never believed I was inferior to anybody else, even though some blacks said it and white society insisted on it.

I developed a hatred for whites, angry at the accumulation of racially motivated attitudes and incidents I saw around me. For a time during these years whenever I saw a white person, I automatically frowned and clenched my fists, but I never dared express my feelings out loud. If I had, I knew I would have received a whipping, either from some white person or from a relative. White society assumed the validity of black subservience, and my relatives had internalized society's attitudes and had come to accept their own subordination and segregation. I had no choice but to go along with the system, but I never accepted its premises internally; soon I realized that my anti-white feelings were actually demeaning to me.

I believe there were several reasons why I was able to come to these conclusions. Despite what I have said about my mother's attitudes, I believe she instilled values in me that prevented me from accepting any ideas of inferiority. Though she insisted that we had to be humble toward whites, she also let us know that we were special. She taught us that we had worth; we were somebody.

In school there was some black history instruction, though it mainly consisted of pictures of black heroes on our classroom walls. I knew of blacks who had accomplished something. I knew of Booker T. Washington; I knew of his conflict with W. E. B. DuBois (I thought DuBois was right). I heard of Marcus Garvey's work in the cities. I particularly admired Frederick Douglass. To me, he personified standing up for yourself and others. He said to black people: "You're as great as anyone else, and don't think you aren't." It was inspiring to know of a black man who did not accept discrimination and, more important, did not accept the arguments of inferiority which supported that discrimination.

Another reason for my refusal to accept ideas of inferiority was my chance to see a role model in my own community. Most blacks I knew during my childhood worked at menial jobs in the lumberyard or in other businesses around town. The height of black ambition at that time was to become a teacher or a minister. When I moved in with my aunt and uncle, they lived near the town's only black doctor, Dr. Charles Smith. I went to him with minor illnesses a couple of times, though usually our family depended on home remedies. I never knew him very well; he was a distant person I occasionally saw on my way to school. When I saw him, he was friendly, but we had absolutely no personal relationship. As I passed his house on my way to and from school, I would see his fine home, his finely manicured lawn, and I would say to myself: "My goodness, that's the way to live." I saw a black man who seemed to have gained material success, and I dreamed it might be possible for me too.

*Dr. Charles W. Smith, top row, far right, the
young Douglas Conner's role model and inspiration*

From my earliest time, I can remember wanting to become a doctor, my experience with Dr. Smith only inten-
sifying an already existing feeling. I can remember as a
very young child soaking red and green paper in water to
produce red and green liquid. I put this colored water into
bottles and pretended it was my medicine. The suffering I
saw around me also intensified my desire. I often told
myself I would become a doctor and remedy this suffering. I particularly remember being affected by the death of
a pregnant young girl in our neighborhood. Someone had
tried to abort the pregnancy, and she died as a result of the
lack of proper medical care.

I never discussed my ambition with my parents or with

16

relatives. When I told my childhood friends, they looked at me in disbelief. My mother always told us that, whatever we wanted to do or to be, we should put forward our best effort. If we did, she said, we could do it. I early set my sights on becoming a physician, and I kept at it. My dreaming about it kept my hopes up and prevented me from accepting a subordinate role all my life.

The fact that I was able to attend and finish high school was also significant. Most black boys my age dropped out of school to go to work. The generosity of my aunt and uncle and my working after school and during summers as a dishwasher, mopper, and cleaner at white cafés allowed me to stay in school. I was also fortunate to have had dedicated teachers who demanded performance from me and my schoolmates. (I attended Eureka High School from the sixth to the twelfth grade, the school being about a mile from where I lived with my relatives.) In the sixth grade there was Miss Henry, with her friendly, smiling approach to learning; in the seventh grade Miss Cora Jones taught with the aid of a thick strap; in the eighth grade Miss Clark taught with kindness. In high school Professor Whissington taught me chemistry, and I marveled at the experiments he was able to perform without the proper equipment. He inspired in me a love of science which was so essential for my later medical training.

All my life I had been quite introverted, reading books or magazines my mother and aunt obtained for me instead of playing, holding in thoughts rather than expressing them. Several of my teachers recognized my need to come out of myself and urged me to participate in the dramatic club. I had only bit parts, but these experiences accustomed me to speaking before crowds and getting out of myself. High school was a growing experience for me; I learned a great deal and I also learned to express myself in public. Completing high school gave me a feeling of ac-

Douglas Conner, 1939 graduate of Eureka High School, Hattiesburg

complishment most black youths my age did not experience.

During these years I also had an opportunity to read black newspapers. I was able to buy the Pittsburgh *Courier* and the Chicago *Defender* from people in the neighborhood who were agents for the papers. (During high school I sold the *Courier* myself.) I learned of black people outside my circle; I learned there was a black (and white) world outside my experience. Every time I read an issue of one of these papers, however, I became angry. The stories about some white person shooting a black person or doing some other violence were upsetting. I kept asking myself why I continued reading the papers when they disturbed me so much, but I kept reading them, and I believe they too had an influence on me.

The radio was another window on the world. I can't remember listening to any specific program except for *Amos and Andy*. The program made me laugh but at the same time it made me mad. I disliked the way it portrayed black people. Still I found myself listening to it. At the least, the radio provided me with another alternative to the stultifying atmosphere of Hattiesburg segregation.

By the time I graduated from high school in 1939 as the class salutatorian, two things were set in my mind: I was going to be a doctor, and I was not willing to accept the system of segregation that kept blacks like me submerged. My thoughts were not all that clear at the time, but perhaps deep inside I thought I could become a physician to serve black people and help bring them hope. I did nothing to battle discrimination at that time because I was too busy just surviving. My goal was college. Armed with my diploma, a fifty-dollar scholarship in my hand, and ten dollars from my mother in my pocket, I planned to attend the black state school in Mississippi, Alcorn A and M.

19

2

THE ALCORN YEARS

When I think back today on Alcorn A and M, I realize how fortunate I was to attend the school, let alone complete four years of study and graduate. All my life I had thought of becoming a doctor, and I knew I had to go to college if I was to reach that goal. However, at that time not many graduates of Eureka High School were able to go on to higher education. The others had to take jobs to make a living. I was one of only eight people from my graduating class who went on to college.

Since my grades were good, I did not have any academic problems with admission to the four black Mississippi schools open to me: Tougaloo, Rust, Alcorn, and Jackson College. My problems were financial. Tougaloo, for example, was a private school, at that time considered the top black school in the state. It was the place for middle-class blacks who could afford the tuition. Low-income blacks like me normally did not even bother to apply there because it was beyond our financial reach. Therefore, I never considered Tougaloo or either of the other black schools. State-operated Alcorn was my only choice. In those days Alcorn awarded fifty-dollar scholarships each year to the valedictorian and salutatorian of every black high school in the state. Upon graduation I received the salutatorian grant. The following summer I continued working in a downtown café and earned enough money to buy myself some fairly decent clothes. My mother and my aunt and uncle also provided some financial help and encouragement. I don't remember how much money I gathered, but I do remember that after I bought my Greyhound bus ticket for the trip from Hattiesburg to Alcorn all I had was fifteen dollars plus the fifty-dollar scholarship. When I boarded the bus that day in September 1939, this little money and a small suitcase was all I owned. I did not realize it then, but I would never live in Hattiesburg again.

It might have been different had it not been for segregation. The school that today is called the University of Southern Mississippi is located in Hattiesburg, and had I been white I might have gone there. But I never gave it any thought. In those days blacks had no connection with Southern. It was a totally different world. I never remember even going on the campus; none of my teachers took any of our classes there for programs. Segregation was so severe in Hattiesburg that no black person thought about any relationship with the school except in some menial capacity.

The bus I took from Hattiesburg did not go to the Alcorn campus. It stopped at the now famous nearby general store on Highway 61 in Lorman. The college provided transportation the rest of the way. I don't remember much about the bus ride, but I vividly remember my first impressions of Alcorn. We traveled down a winding unpaved road through a thick forest, and I wondered where in the backwoods I was going. Suddenly the school bus went around yet another bend in the road and I saw a group of buildings and tall oak trees with moss hanging from the branches. I felt as though I had entered another world. What a beautiful place, I thought. Today, one must take this same winding road through the same woods, and the impression is still one of serene, isolated beauty. I did not think of it at the time, but I had indeed entered another world, as cut off from the outside as any place could be. As I looked around me with all the wonder only a freshman can feel, I had no such grand thoughts. Instead, I worried about the condition of my finances.

The cost of attending Alcorn that year was $62.50. Since I had the $50 scholarship and $15 in my pocket, my visit to the school's fiscal office left me with only $2.50. I was assigned to the men's freshman dormitory, Mississippi Hall, and found I was sharing a second-floor room with seven other freshmen. The 20-foot by 20-foot room was furnished with four double-deck beds and had one closet. I spent little time contemplating the situation. I began looking for a job on campus.

Fortunately I was able to find a job cleaning the first floor of Bowles Hall, one of the instructional buildings. I held that job for part of a year, until I became assistant to the dean of men of Mississippi Hall, a position I held for the rest of my stay at Alcorn. I did some cleaning, but mostly I carried letters to other buildings on campus and generally helped supervise the students in the dormitory. During my junior year I was also given the task of ringing the bell that announced class changes. I attended my own classes, keeping a sharp eye on my watch, then left each class five minutes early and rushed over to Oakland Chapel to ring the bell to signal the end of that class period. I did this every hour on the hour for two years.

During my years at Alcorn the campus consisted of eleven buildings arranged in a large oval pattern along a similarly oval street. There were men's and women's dormitories, instructional buildings, the president's home, faculty residences, and a student hospital. Two other buildings were particularly central to student life. In the middle of the oval stood the dining hall, a large wooden structure that was reached by walking from the dormitories down the hill past the moss-filled oak trees. Along one side of the oval near the Administration Building and the president's home was Oakland Chapel, built by the Presbyterians who had operated the college which preceded Alcorn on the site. This historic building provided facilities both for religious services and for any other activities that required the students to be together in one place.

Of all the buildings on campus, Mississippi Hall stands out in my mind over and above the rest. I spent my impressionable first year there, but I also worked there during most of my college career. I remember it as being an imposing structure, one of the oldest on campus, probably even more impressive to someone like me who had never before seen anything quite like it.

The atmosphere in Mississippi Hall was, I imagine, no different from that in any other dormitory on any other college campus during recent times. It was noisy and crowded. One difference was that, unlike today's college dormitories, Mississippi Hall had no special facilities for studying. There was no place to study except in the lobby which, needless to say, was even noisier than the corridors where the rooms were located. There were no desks in the rooms, and the only way to read was to lie on a bunk and try to squint at a book under the single overhead light in the middle of the ceiling. Having eight people in one room also made studying very difficult. After the first several weeks, however, we learned that all eight of us were seldom in the room at the same time except when we were sleeping. Still, the atmosphere was sometimes so noisy that the only way I could concentrate on my studies was to stick my fingers in my ears to muffle the racket. I never studied in the college library because its hours were limited and it was viewed as a research source, not as a study area.

Mississippi Hall, Alcorn A and M College: Douglas Conner lived and worked here as a student

I was very fortunate to have seven compatible room-mates. During my first several weeks in the room I often wished for more privacy, but as all of us got to know each other better we learned that there was no need for pre-tense; we could just be ourselves. After that, I did not mind the situation nearly as much. The eight of us got along so well that we remained friends through out college and into later life. For example, I still consider Reuben Morris, a Pascagoula physician, and Richard Daugherty, a Chicago dentist, to be my friends.

None of us, with the exception of Daugherty, had many clothes. He came from a fairly middle-class black family, and he had several suits, a luxury the rest of us did not enjoy. So all eight of us shared his clothes. He was shorter

24

than the rest of us, and the clothes did not fit us perfectly. Still, an undersized suit was better than nothing. Sometimes the situation became humorous. One of the others might wear a suit to chapel, and then I might wear the same suit to dinner. A mutual friend would comment that the suit sure looked familiar; hadn't he already seen it somewhere else that day? Daugherty's trousers were at least an inch too short for me, but whenever I was questioned I always feigned ignorance. After other students figured out exactly what was going on, the question I often heard was: "Just who does that suit belong to, you or Daugherty?"

Most of the time I was not concerned about the ownership of clothes. Attending classes and making grades were my major preoccupations. I was working toward a Bachelor of General Science degree, so I took a heavy load of science courses—chemistry, biology, and so forth. I usually spent about five hours a day in class. I found the all-black faculty to be excellent. Several stick out in my mind. Mr. Hearst, my chemistry instructor, was the sort of person who kept pushing and pushing until he was sure everyone understood clearly what he was saying. He seemed to feel offended if the whole class did not understand everything. My English teacher, Mrs. Murdock, was a very proper lady who insisted on very proper English. The teacher who taught me world and European history, Mr. Charles Wilson, really knew his subject and used humor to get it across to us. When I took French and German, Miss Henrietta Levi related her experiences in Paris as a way of helping us learn. In later years, as I was going through medical school and then practicing medicine, I came to appreciate my Alcorn education. To this day I believe I received a first-rate education during the four years I was an Alcorn student.

I also maintained a busy schedule outside the classroom.

During my sophomore year I began learning how to play the saxophone, and during my last two years, I was a member of the 100-piece marching band under the direction of Mr. Kermit Holly. For about a year I sang in the college chorus which was directed by Mrs. William H. Bell, the wife of our efficient college president. She had the ability to conduct without a lot of arm-waving. She merely gave an appropriate glance and the chorus reacted accordingly. I was also elected in my senior year to be editor of the student newspaper, the *Greater Alcorn Herald*. I wrote editorials about school life, but I can't remember any specific topics. Unfortunately the issues from those years have not been preserved, so there is no way of finding out the subjects of my editorials.

I continued to be an active churchgoer during my Alcorn years, regularly attending the Sunday morning services conducted by the college chaplain, Miss Lucretta Wright. The services were interdenominational. Miss Wright was such a forceful speaker that she could keep me spellbound for thirty or forty minutes and also defuse any criticism about being a woman. There were no mandatory religious services, at least in theory, but in practice students were expected to go to chapel every Sunday.

Sports also played a major role in my life and that of every other Alcorn student during those years. I played no varsity sports, but I was a member of intramural teams in basketball and volleyball and enjoyed watching the varsity teams in action. The major sports during my day were basketball and football. There was always a great deal of fanfare surrounding every home football game, including a big parade into the stadium. Homecoming was even more spectacular. I attended most of the games on campus and even went to Jackson one year for a game against our archrival, Tougaloo. Most of the time, however, students did not go to games played away. We had to learn the result by word of mouth after the team had returned to campus.

The other forms of recreation on campus were card playing, talking to the girls, after-game gatherings, and hops or dances. Our dances were certainly different from the kind young people enjoy today. Our music was a lot slower and less frantic. I can best describe it as Duke Ellington–Count Basie music.

Looking back on my four years at Alcorn, one of the things that strikes me now is how completely I became part of the campus. I in fact rarely left. I never went home for Christmas because it was too expensive to make the trip and because I did not feel I had a real family to return to. Since few others stayed, Alcorn was a lonely place during the holiday season. I usually only went to my aunt and uncle's home for a week or so during summers, and the rest of the time I continued in my job as assistant to the Mississippi Hall dean of men. Dean Frank Christmas was gone frequently, so I was often acting dean of men, quite a responsibility for an undergraduate. Mr. Christmas was a musician, in fact headed the school orchestra, and he often took the group off campus to play for dances. The students who played in this group were among the few who were able to leave campus with any regularity. The rest of us could leave only for extraordinary reasons, except during scheduled vacation times.

As I noted earlier, the campus was another world, insulated from most exterior influences. We knew there was a society out there, because we had come from it and were planning to return to some part of it one day, but while we were at Alcorn we really did not feel a part of the world outside it. One advantage of living in an all-black society cut off from most connections with the dominant white world was our temporary opportunity to avoid the blight of segregation. There were no whites around to remind us

27

to watch our racial P's and Q's. We could be relaxed since we did not have to worry about violating racial mores and getting into trouble. We could be ourselves and forget the kind of society from from which we had come.

But perhaps this forgetting was not all that good. We students grew quite content with our situation. There was no acute sensitivity to the issue of segregation at Alcorn as there was at Jackson-based Tougaloo or at Jackson College. For a time I considered switching to one of these schools and putting myself into the middle of things. I sometimes worried about having the world pass me by, about Rip Van Winkling my time away, but I knew I could not afford to transfer, so I put such ideas out of my mind. And, like everyone else, I was lulled into forgetting about segregation. It was as though the problem did not exist. The only professor who ever talked about it to us was our outspoken history instructor, Mr. Wilson, although he never said much about black history or the roots of segregation.

It was not that we students thought the problem had gone away, but in our frequent conversations on being black in Mississippi we talked in the following terms: "Give me a chance. I don't want you to give me anything, just give me a chance. Let me be able to advance as well as anyone else." Having said that, someone would usually express the hope, really the belief, that our education would make a difference and lessen the discrimination against us once we graduated.

We students at Alcorn and my friends and relatives in Hattiesburg accepted the existence of segregation and discrimination, but there was a difference in our attitudes toward it. Dealing with it every day, blacks who lived in white society became fatalistic and saw no real hope for the future. We students at Alcorn, living in an all-black world away from whites, believed our education would make a difference. We saw our future as providing leadership for black people within the context of a segregated society. We hoped our leadership would produce an improvement for all blacks, but, even if it did not, we thought our education would at least make our own lives a little more tolerable. (Significantly, we never talked about voting.)

Though we lived this relatively comfortable life at Alcorn, we could not totally isolate ourselves from the outside world. World War II was raging, and it frequently impinged on all of us. More and more Alcorn students were volunteering for service. (By the time I graduated in 1943, so many male students had volunteered that Alcorn was almost all female.) For example, Mr. Christmas and the entire orchestra went in as a unit in 1942. Students were normally not drafted, but we still discussed the possibility. We knew that any of us who entered the military would experience segregation, but we did not do much thinking about that. Generally everyone accepted the situation. We expected nothing else from a segregated American society.

We spent more time thinking and talking about the racism of our enemy—one of our enemies—Nazi Germany. Whenever we talked about the war and what the fighting was all about, someone would mention Hitler and his racist attitude toward blacks. We had no doubt about Hitler's prejudice because we had all heard the story about his snub of Jesse Owens during the 1936 Olympic Games. It never dawned on us that there was a real irony in the fact that the United States was trying to eradicate Nazi racism with a military formed along racist principles.

At Alcorn we knew nothing about A. Philip Randolph and his threatened march on Washington in 1941. We also knew little if anything about President Roosevelt's executive order which established the Fair Employment Practices Commission (FEPC). But we did know about the

naming of the first black general, Benjamin O. Davis. I
don't remember whether we used the phrase then, but I
know we considered Davis's promotion a token gesture.
Still, we saw the move as a step in the right direction and
rejoiced that a black man had made history by reaching the
rank of general.

My lack of knowledge of many contemporary events
during my college years was the result of several circumstances. Alcorn's isolated site allowed us to forget the outside world all too often. I remember the library receiving
newspapers, but I don't remember the *Defender* or the
Courier being available. I was also so busy during these
years working, studying, or going to class that I paid less
attention to world events than I should have. I had not lost
my curiosity, but lack of time and lack of campus stimulation kept me more uninformed than I care to remember.

I have mentioned that during my Alcorn years I made a
number of friends and that several professors made a last-
ing impression on me. But there were two people of all
those I knew at Alcorn who made the most significant
marks on my life. One of these I knew only in passing; the
other one became my wife. I will discuss my marriage to
Juanita in more detail later on, but I want to mention her
here in my discussion of Alcorn because it was there that
we met and fell in love. I had been dating several other
girls, none of them very seriously, when one day during
my junior year I happened to look out one of the windows
in Mississippi Hall and noticed a girl passing by. She was
very thin and held her head in the air in such a way that her
long hair flowed down her back. I watched her walk
around the building toward the faculty housing in the
street behind. After that first time I often saw her walk by,
and I watched her from outside the building until she was
out of sight. Finally I got up enough courage to meet her
and walk with her as she hurried to her job as domestic for

my English teacher, Mrs. Murdock. After several such encounters, she let me walk her back to her dormitory. My big concern was her boyfriend; I'll never forget his name—Grover. I had to beat Grover's time, and it was not an easy task. Finally, though, I replaced Grover, and Juanita and I became closer and closer. Eventually we were to marry.

In addition to Juanita, the college physician had an important impact on me, similar to that of Dr. Charles Smith in Hattiesburg. (By coincidence, the campus physician was a brother of the Dr. Smith in my hometown.) I never became close to either man, but both inspired me simply by their examples. I had to work to stay in school, and my studies and other activities kept me so busy that I never spent any time around the college hospital. Thinking back and remembering my passion for medicine, I wonder why I did not make a greater effort to get to know Dr. Luther Smith. The only time I really saw him was during my own physical and when, on several occasions, I had to take sick students to his four-bed campus hospital. At those times I was able to see him in action, and his quiet expertise made a profound impression on me. It increased my determination to be a doctor myself one day. I never told him of his effect on me; he hardly said a word to me, but his influence was real nonetheless.

My college years passed quickly, and I received my degree in June 1943. I had a "B" average for my four years' work, finishing in the upper third of my class, but I won no academic honors as I had in high school. Earlier in my college career I had won an oratorical contest at Alcorn and had competed for a scholarship in a state contest in Jackson sponsored by a leading black businessman, S. R. Redmond. I finished second, and the only prize I received was congratulations. I often think that I should have done better scholastically while in college, but all my involvements outside of class kept my grades down. Still, my performance was most respectable under the circumstances.

These years at Alcorn were a crucial time in my life. Coming out of a broken home as I did and increasingly separated from my family, I developed for the first time a sense of belonging, of togetherness. During my Alcorn years I had very little contact with my family. My mother wrote regularly a couple of times each month (each time generously enclosing several dollars from her meager finances), but we did not see much of each other until I began my medical practice in 1951. From then until her death in 1970, we were together five to six times a year. While at Alcorn I spent only about a week each summer with my aunt and uncle and sometimes did not see my mother at all because she was living in Picayune. I could not afford to visit home more often than that, and an extra trip to Picayune was financially out of the question. On graduation day no one from my family could afford to attend, and I understood. As it was, I had come to view the Alcorn community as my new family. Before I came there my life had been a series of zig and zags; at Alcorn, with its rural setting and its lack of outside distractions, I was able to find my bearings. I grew content because I felt a part of something.

Had Alcorn been a predominantly white school, I'm not sure I would have felt the same way. There was something special about being part of an all-black world—a world populated and controlled by blacks. I saw blacks in positions of authority and respect; I held positions of the same kind. It was something I had rarely seen in the outside world. There, most of the blacks around me held menial jobs, were given little if any respect, and had almost no hope for future improvement. At Alcorn there was hope because we saw clearly that, despite white insistence, blacks were capable of learning, of leadership, of respect. The whole atmosphere was positive, and I was part of it. It felt wonderful. We lacked the equipment and the faculty prestige of white institutions, but that was not the crucial fact. We had pride in ourselves and what we were doing. We recognized concretely the myth of white-imposed black inferiority. We believe that once we graduated we would help destroy that myth.

As important as the education I received at Alcorn was to me—and I am convinced that it was excellent—I believe the togetherness and the family feeling I gained there were even more important. If I had to do it again today, I would again go to Alcorn. At the same time, I must admit that I would be tempted to go to one of the integrated schools such as Mississippi State University or Ole Miss or Southern. These universities have much better facilities, more prestigious faculties, and greater reputations than the predominantly black schools in Mississippi because they have consistently received larger shares of state funds. Many black students are attending these schools today. (My own son was the first black student at Mississippi State.) I believe in and fought for integration, so I am happy to see black students at formerly all-white universities.

But I worry too. I know black students are getting a good education when they go to a predominantly white school, but I wonder whether they are experiencing the sense of racial togetherness that I gained at Alcorn. I wonder whether they are not receiving irrevocable insults to their self-esteem. I believe that black college graduates must have a strong sense of obligation to the uplift of the black masses. If black students attend white schools and lose their sense of concern for other blacks, they have lost a golden opportunity.

Unconcern is one thing, but even more disturbing is the black graduate of the white school who gains an education

33

and in the process develops a superior attitude toward less-privileged blacks. I have seen too many instances of such people taking the attitude: "If you work as hard as I have, you'll make it up here too." Any blacks who believe they have made it on their own are sadly mistaken. Without the selfless sacrifice of so many before them, today's black students would still be suffering under the same segregation that was for so long a way of life in Mississippi. They would not be sitting in classrooms at the state's predominantly white institutions.

Even worse than these individuals are those black graduates of white institutions who have developed a repugnance for less-privileged blacks. Instead of trying to work together to uplift the masses, they take the attitude: "Those trifling people, they ought to be ashamed of themselves for being poor and uneducated and downtrodden." Unfortunately I have seen a great many black graduates take on this attitude, and I believe this is the result of their never developing any group cohesiveness, any togetherness, during their college days. They have become "Oreo cookie" types: they are black on the outside, but their insides are white. They have learned much technical information at the white universities, but they have also learned to separate themselves from their black brothers and sisters. What a waste of human potential!

My experience at Alcorn was totally different. I learned to be a part of a group working together for black betterment. I would not exchange that experience for anything.

I had two other experiences during these years that were also important in forming my later life. In the summer between my junior and senior years and in the year immediately after graduation I traveled, for the first time, outside the South. During the summer of 1942 I worked on a tobacco farm in Connecticut, and for almost a year—from June 1943 to May 1944—I worked in an automobile plant in Detroit, Michigan. Considering my limited life in small-town Mississippi and isolated Alcorn, going North was a real adventure.

During my junior year some recruiters came on the campus looking for students to work on the tobacco farm in Connecticut. They offered to furnish all the transportation up and back, provide housing, and pay wages besides. The job called for picking the tobacco leaves and taking them to appropriate sheds for curing. No experience was necessary, the recruiters told us—we would be taught all we needed to know once we got there. It sounded good to me, and I agreed to go. Approximately twenty other students also signed up and a professor agreed to go as adviser.

We left during the middle of June 1942, sometime after classes were out for the year. I did not go back to Hattiesburg, but merely wrote my family to tell them of my plans. By now I was on my own, and no longer felt it necessary to get anyone's permission to do anything. My mother wrote back and asked only that I write and tell her what I was doing once I got there.

I don't remember the route we took to get to the farm, which was located between Hartford and the Massachusetts state line somewhere near the town of Windsor. I remember the bus stopping in several large cities, but since I never left the bus depot, I did not get a chance to see much. The tobacco farm was enormous. We lived in three furnished houses, each house two stories high. These were fairly decent places, and the twenty of us plus the faculty adviser found them to be pleasant. We had to pay for our own food out of our earnings, but we never had to pay for anything else. I don't remember what our wages were, but it was a lot of money to us. There were no places nearby where we could spend our money, so it went a lot further than it might have had we been closer to a populated area.

I quickly noted something I had not seen before. We Alcorn blacks worked side by side with white laborers from the area. Even more unusual than this integration was the fact that all the white workers were Polish. They spoke very little English, and it was difficult for us to communicate with them at first, but I learned some Polish and they learned some English and we communicated enough to be able to work together efficiently. The second amazing thing was that these Polish people, who were good hard-working common laborers, did not seem to have a prejudiced bone in their bodies. I never saw even a hint of prejudice. They treated us as they treated each other. Even the foremen and subforemen exhibited a good attitude. As a southern black man, I had become accustomed to having white people treat me in a condescending manner at best. Here I came face to face with white people who dealt with me in a person-to-person manner rather than in a master-to-slave manner. It was an eye-opening experience to see that whites did not necessarily have to be prejudicial in their treatment of blacks.

The Polish workers did not live on the farm, but commuted daily from Connecticut and Massachusetts. Most of the time we never left the farm. We worked from early morning until five in the afternoon, Monday through Friday. Saturdays and Sundays we were off, and we also had a generous break for lunch on workdays. When we were not working, we played ball or cards, read, or just talked. Once in a while our faculty adviser would drive a group of us into Hartford in a farm car. Again, we experienced no discrimination that I can remember.

Looking back now, the most important thing about my tobacco farm work (which, by the way, I found interesting) was this contact with whites who treated me on terms of equality. At the time, however, the money I earned was more important to me than any insights into human nature. By the time we returned to Alcorn in the middle of September, I had saved about $300—more money than I had ever had before. I also brought back with me a "zoot suit" which I had purchased in Hartford during one of my visits into the city. I quickly realized that what was stylish in Hartford was not necessarily stylish in Mississippi, and soon cast off my one concrete souvenir of northern life. However, I never forgot those Polish people and the lesson they taught me about human relations.

When I graduated from Alcorn, the good money and the better climate of race relations turned me toward the North again. Having finished college, my next step on the road toward my M.D. degree was medical school. As always, the problem was money. I simply did not have the funds to go to medical school at Meharry College in Nashville or Howard University in Washington. (I never considered anywhere else; I thought these two black schools were my only hope.) Sometime during my senior year at Alcorn I decided to go to Detroit to work for a year or two and earn enough money to finance my medical education. I had heard there was plenty of work in Detroit, so I set my sights on going there rather than to Chicago, St. Louis, or somewhere else. Somehow I had decided that Detroit would be more like Mississippi than anyplace else I might go. I had also read so many negative things about life in Chicago in the Chicago *Defender* that I never seriously considered going there.

Before leaving in late June 1943 I spent a week with Uncle Tom and Aunt Lillian, and these two wonderful people helped me with the fare to Detroit and encouraged me in my plans. They also gave me the name and address of a woman they knew in Detroit. Other than that name and a few clothes, I took nothing else with me when I boarded the bus to try to make my fortune in the North.

When I arrived I immediately looked up my aunt's

Douglas Conner in 1943, after graduation from Alcorn

friend, and she helped me find a place to rent, a bedroom in a very large house. Two other renters also lived there, and they had kitchen privileges in addition to their bedrooms. I rented only the room and ate all my meals in nearby cafés. I don't remember the name of the street where I lived, but it was in a black neighborhood and fairly near the Mack Avenue Fisher Body plant of General

Motors, where I found a job by answering a newspaper ad.

I became a common laborer. I did not work on the assembly line, but instead spent my time getting parts in position for use on the line. It was not difficult work, and I caught onto it very quickly—perhaps too quickly. One of my first days on the job I was working at what I thought was an ordinary pace. A white union steward watched me for a few minutes and with a smile on his face came over to my side. "Hey, buddy, you're from Mississippi, aren't you?" "Sure am," I replied. "Well," he said, "up here, we don't work that fast. You're breakin' your neck. Just take it easy."

All this was said in a friendly way, as was a later invitation to join the union, a part of the CIO. Any time a new person began work at the plant, he was approached about joining up. The union was very strong in that factory. There was no strike during the time I worked there but if a worker had any problem he went to the union steward and it wasn't long before the problem was corrected. The union played a positive role, so I readily joined and remained a member.

More whites than blacks worked in the factory, and a generally friendly atmosphere prevailed. There were no open signs of discrimination or racial animosity on the job. Everyone was "one of the gang" during work hours, but once the factory whistle blew, everything changed—the same fellows who were so pleasant during work time suddenly ignored me if they ran into me on the way home. In the South I was used to blatant racism; this kind of hypocrisy confused me. Detroiters seemed to pretend that everyone was the same, but discrimination of a subtle kind was clearly present. From my experience in Connecticut and from reading the Chicago *Defender* and the Pittsburgh *Courier*, I had an inflated idea about race relations in the

North. Certainly things were better in the North; segregation was not as total, nor discrimination as brutal, but blacks and whites did live in separate neighborhoods in Detroit, and they seldom met outside the workplace. I had no problems in stores or theaters, and I don't remember blacks in Detroit talking as much about discrimination as blacks in the South did. I noticed they were more carefree and less fearful than southern blacks. They seemed to sense less impending doom than blacks in the South. But the Detroit riot of 1943 indicated that things were not perfect, and my own experiences showed me antiblack prejudice was present. (I have no remembrance of the riot because it did not affect the neighborhood I lived in, or my job. I don't even remember much discussion about it.)

When I first arrived in Detroit, the size of the city overwhelmed me. It was the biggest thing I had ever seen. After I had been there for a while, however, I came to see it not as one large entity, but as a collection of little towns—a congregation of little Hattiesburgs. The war had made it into a boom town. Everyone seemed to be working and while they worked they talked about the war. The war was the leading topic of conversation everywhere I went.

I worked a 40-hour week in the automobile factory and spent most of my spare time reading in my room. I mostly read magazines like *Reader's Digest,* but I also purchased a few medical books. I did not establish any regimen of study and simply kept up my interest in medicine by occasionally reading about anatomy and other similar subjects. Sometimes I would go to a movie, or I would simply walk around. I went to a neighborhood Baptist church fairly regularly, and found it more formal than the southern Baptist churches I was used to. I also found the pace of life in Detroit much faster than what I was used to. I thought at the time that I would never like to spend my life in a city. There was too much rush, rush, rush. I could not imagine life being very enjoyable under such conditions.

After about a year in Detroit I realized that I was not saving as much money as I had hoped. My rent and food expenses proved to be greater than I had expected. In May 1944 I was saved from having to make a decision whether or not to stay another year: I was drafted. The year in Detroit had brought me a few new clothes and several hundred dollars, hardly enough to get me into any medical school. My entrance into the service moved me closer to medical school than another year or two in the Detroit automobile plant ever would have. It proved to be a blessing in disguise, though at the time I did not realize it.

However, the year in Detroit was a good experience for me. I tasted life in the city; I came to get a better view of northern race relations; and I came into contact with a great many different people. On the job I learned the importance of people working together, cooperating with each other, toiling in the same spirit. Once again, too, I saw blacks and whites working together on a more or less equal footing. The whole thing had a broadening effect on me. As in Connecticut, my hopes were buoyed: black-white relations were not as ironclad as everyone in Mississippi thought and said they were.

My four years at Alcorn, the summer in Connecticut, and the year in Detroit were all part of the educational process. Alcorn opened me to the possibility of black togetherness; Connecticut and Detroit broadened my horizons to worlds I had never been aware of before. Alcorn had been a closed world, as had Connecticut. Detroit was a white-dominated big city, the world in its brashest form. I found that, as a black man, I was not automatically excluded. I could participate, and I could survive. This was an important lesson for the future.

3
ARMY LIFE

From the time the draft was instituted during World War II, I was classified 1-A. Fortunately I was allowed to conclude my college education before I was called. Draft boards usually tried to permit students to complete a school year before inducting them, but students were sometimes called in the middle of a semester. As it turned out, I was not called until a year after graduation, late April, early May 1944, near the end of my year in Detroit. I entered the service that June.

Although my draft notice came from Hattiesburg, I was not sent to nearby Camp Shelby, where so many Alcorn people had gone. Instead, I was ordered to report to Fort Sheridan, Illinois. I was probably one of the few Mississippi draftees at that midwestern military post.

Several thoughts raced through my mind as I rode the bus full of Detroit draftees from the Motor City to Fort Sheridan. First of all, I had mixed emotions about entering the military. I of course had no idea what sort of a job the military would give me, or where they would send me. I worried about going into a combat zone and dying in battle. At the same time, I hoped that somehow I might receive a medical position and improve my chances of entering medical school. I believed firmly that my service would entitle me to some sort of veteran's benefits. The G.I. Bill was a thing of the future, but I was confident that the government would provide all veterans with postwar help and I would be able to use this money to finance my medical education.

I also thought about the segregated military I was entering. Again, I had ambivalent thoughts. It galled me to think of entering a racist institution, but I tried to soften my anger by viewing the matter from a broader perspective. I told myself: "This is my country too, and even though I don't like the idea of fighting for it under humiliating circumstances, it's still worth fighting for. Maybe somewhere down the road, at another time, this segregation business can be solved." In short, I entered the army feeling it my duty to serve my country in wartime. I was also determined to help demonstrate that being black did not automatically mean being an inferior, shiftless, no-good individual. I had high hopes that military service might prove beneficial for me and for blacks generally.

My initial army experience was typically cold and impersonal. After we received our uniforms and equipment, we draftees were told to strip for our physicals. We were probed, poked, and examined. My clearest memory is walking between two long rows of army medics—and they were all bruisers—to get my shots. The hypodermic needles seemed to be flying from every direction, and I remember thinking that the bruisers were getting too much delight out of administering the shots. I noticed too that they and all the doctors were white; all of us going through the line were black. I saw, from the start, that segregation was indeed a part of the army's standard operating procedure.

I stayed at Fort Sheridan only a few weeks, mostly waiting around. Finally, a group of us were shipped to Camp

43

Barclay, in southwest Texas, for basic training. And it was tough. We were on the move from dawn to past dusk under the watchful eyes of a corps of white officers and a black sergeant who was our drill instructor. The sergeant was fully capable of handling our 150-man company. He was most skilled in talking loud and getting all of us to follow his instructions. My life became a round of training, inspections, drill, and policing the area. It was exhausting.

Camp Barclay housed both white and black troops, but we took no training together. We blacks never even got close enough to the white troops to know whether our training and theirs was identical. After hours, most of us were so tired we had little thought of anything except our bunks, and those were segregated too. Sometime in the middle of basic we were allowed to leave the post for the first time. There was a small town nearby where we went to forget the rigorous training for a while. There too we had no contact with whites; they went to the white areas of town and we went to the black ones. Only the white MPs caused us any problems. Many were Simon Legrees, similar to police officers I had seen all too often in the South. Some of them swung their billy clubs too quickly, and every once in a while a black skull suffered the consequences.

There were a handful of black MPs, but there were no black officers. All my time in the army I never saw a black officer. Every one of my commanders was white. I must say, though, that most of them were pretty decent people. None ever talked to me directly about the segregation of black and white soldiers, but at times I got the feeling that they did not like the idea. However, most of them were career officers, and they did what they were told to do. Segregation was what the army wanted, so whether they liked it or not they were not going to question it.

44

Throughout my basic training I kept trying to think of ways to foster my interest in medicine. I dreamed about entering a medical unit in the army; I had heard stories of men advancing through the ranks right into medical school. I hoped, but, deep down, I never believed I had much chance. Blacks like me were always the last considered for anything American society offered.

Sometime during basic training I came across a notice about medical training for enlisted men at Walter Reed Army Hospital in Washington. I immediately went to my superiors, and they allowed me to take a test which determined candidates for this training. I was fortunate enough to be chosen. Eight of us from Barclay were put on a train for Washington and from July 7 to September 2, 1944, we were enrolled in the "Enlisted Specialist course for Surgical Technicians" at the army's premier hospital.

Walter Reed Army Hospital was, during the war, an even larger complex than it is today. It was simply enormous. I was so excited about being there that I remember little except finding my living quarters and marveling at the size of the facility. My astonishment only increased when we began classes. Our living quarters were arranged according to the usual segregation, but our classes and our work in the wards were not. There were approximately one hundred of us enrolled in the course. The group picture of the class shows eight black faces sprinkled in among the whites, and that was the way it was with everything connected with the course. We blacks were thoroughly integrated with the much more numerous whites. The instructors never said anything about it (several blacks even taught us), none of the white students made any comments, and patients in the hospital were similarly silent. Not even the white southerners involved protested. I couldn't believe it. I thought we had to be part of an experiment leading to an integrated army. It was only a

The integrated World War II surgical technicians training course at Walter Reed Army Hospital. Douglas Conner is in the third row from the top, center.

token gesture, of course, but it was much more than I ever expected. (It never occurred to me at the time that the expense and bureaucracy of trying to establish a separate course for black medics may also have been significant in causing this integration.)

I was pleased at this turn of affairs, but I was also somewhat frightened. This was a totally new experience for me. I had never been in the same classroom with whites before, and I worried whether I would be able to measure up to the competition. Would my past education keep me at the bottom of this class? All my life I had been indoctrinated by word and by deed that whites were superior and blacks were inferior. I had never believed it, but after hearing it for so long it was still a part of my psyche. My anxieties were relieved a short while into the course. I discovered that while I was not the brightest student in the class, I was also far from being the dullest. What a relief! I was seeing firsthand what I had always believed. Blacks could successfully compete with whites if only given the chance. It was an exhilarating experience.

I found the course work equally exciting. For the first three weeks we heard lectures on basic anatomy, physiology, and chemistry; all the training was geared toward the practical, toward situations we might run into on the battlefield. Then we were broken down into teams (blacks and whites were mixed together), and we moved into the longest phase of our training, the work with doctors, nurses, and technicians in the hospital. At first we only observed, but soon we were helping out in minor surgeries. Just before we left I even assisted a physician during a major operation. I kept thinking: "Oh my gosh, this is just what I've been dreaming about all my life. Here I am doing it." I couldn't wait to complete the course and to go to some combat zone to put all my knowledge into practice.

The whole experience at Walter Reed was uplifting. I was doing the medical work I had always dreamed of, and I was doing it in an integrated environment I had never dared think was possible. All those around me treated me with respect. I noted that there was no integration during off-duty periods, but I ignored that. It was enough that the military was quietly demonstrating that segregation was not essential for black/white relations. I had no illusions that the classroom integration of eight blacks and some ninety whites would solve the nation's racial problems, but at least I had another reason to hope for better days in the future.

I spent much of my off-duty time studying so that I would do well in the course, but I was also able to see a good deal of Washington. I saw the White House, the Capitol, and many of the other famous sites in the city. Most of the time I went to the black district, to a movie, or simply to look around. (Washington was a southern city when it came to race relations.) I also viewed the seamier side of the city, seeing the kind of slums that most of us try to stay out of. The contrast in Washington was startling: beauty and ugliness existing side by side.

Walter Reed Hospital is not far from Howard University, and I often passed the school during my visits into the city. I remember walking by and hoping that someday Howard would accept me into its medical school. When Howard later did, I was ecstatic. (If Meharry had accepted me first, however, I would have agreed to come immediately. Getting into medical school was more important to me than specifically getting into Howard.)

I made a number of friends during my days in Washington. The eight of us who came from Barclay stayed together for the rest of my military career. After the war several of us attended medical school together. Oswald Nickens is today an orthopedic specialist in Philadelphia, while Lloyd Clayton, though not a physician, is in a medical field.

In retrospect, my experience at Walter Reed was most pleasant. When I left in early September 1944 to return to Camp Barclay, I was more determined than ever to make medicine my life's work. Studying it and watching medical personnel closely convinced me that my goal was the correct one. I sewed my Medical Technician Fifth Class (T-5) insignia on my uniform and made the trip back to Texas, happy with my three months in Washington.

When I returned to Camp Barclay, I joined a medical group attached to the 31st Quartermaster Battalion. During World War II most blacks were put into battalions variously called Quartermaster, Engineer, or Port. Whatever their name, they primarily served one purpose: they provided a place for the army to put black draftees to avoid having to place them in infantry or other combat arms units. There were some black fighting units, but most blacks who participated in the war shared my experience. They were part of service units doing the hard, dirty work of war for the more glamourous and prestigious white combat units.

I did not much care about being kept out of combat, nor did I think about my return to a totally segregated situation. I was too happy with my job as a medic and my chance to put into practice what I had learned at Walter Reed. I worked closely with a white doctor, a white dentist, and other medical people, but I quickly saw that I would not be utilizing most of my recently acquired learning. My job mainly consisted of assisting with sick call. Often I had to use more psychology than medicine. I had to separate the really sick soldiers from those who were only trying to get out of work, and since this unit worked hard, we had more than our share of men hoping for a brief medically approved respite. I was a little disappointed at this lack of more significant activity, but I was pleased to be doing medical work of any kind.

I remained at Barclay until early 1945, when my unit received orders for Okinawa in the Pacific combat zone. All my hopes and fears returned. I wanted to practice my medical training to the fullest, but I did not want to do combat duty. Fortunately I was kept busy enough to keep from mulling about it too much. When I took my two-week furlough in February prior to going with my unit to Seattle for the overseas trip, my family expressed the same concern. My mother openly worried about my not returning. (I saw my father briefly during this visit, but our conversation remained stilted. We exchanged pleasantries and little more.)

During this furlough I became a married man. I had not seen Juanita Macon since my graduation from Alcorn in June 1943, but we had maintained a steady correspondence during my Detroit and army years. We had become very close during our years in school, and our love had grown

49

through the mail. We had begun thinking of marriage sometime during my stay in Detroit, but Nita always insisted on finishing her education first. When I received my orders, I wrote her that I thought we should not wait any longer; we should marry before I went overseas. Fortunately she agreed.

After visiting my family in South Mississippi, I went to Jackson, where Nita joined me. We were married on February 11, 1945, in the Hinds County courthouse. We had made our decision so quickly that a church wedding was impossible and our families were unable to be present. Members of my own family would not have had the money to come under any conditions. (Right after the ceremony Nita's aunt, Sadye Wier, arrived from Starkville. Aunt Sadye had raised Nita, so we were happy she came. This was my first contact with anyone from Nita's family and the beginning of my long and close association with Aunt Sadye.)

To this day, whenever we go to a church wedding, Nita wishes out loud that we had been able to be married in a church. Our honeymoon lasted only three days. We stayed at Lee's Motel near Farish Street in Jackson's black district. We were euphoric about each other, and we tried to concentrate the past years of separation and the uncertain future into this short period. The time went by all too quickly, and I had to return to Texas, while Nita returned to Alcorn. I was greeted with a lot of ribbing from members of my unit, and she was given a shower by her classmates. Nita graduated in June 1945 and that fall began teaching at the Oktibbeha County Training School, the black school in Starkville.

About six weeks after I returned to Camp Barclay, my unit was put on a segregated troop train and shipped to Seattle, arriving sometime in May. There we were put onto a large troopship and began the long Pacific crossing. The crossing was slow and monotonous because the ship zigged and zagged to avoid enemy submarines. There must have been two thousand black and white soldiers on board, but we blacks had little contact with the whites because of segregation.

We had little to do. There was no major organized recreation and there were no training sessions. About the only activity was mandatory calisthenics, which we did by unit on the deck. I never even did any medical work because the ship had its own medical personnel. We killed most of the time in bull sessions. We talked about the war, about where we were going, how dangerous it might or might not be, about our families back home—all the things young men talk about during wartime.

Mainly we wanted the war to be over. The war in Europe had ended that May with the surrender of the Germans, but there was still bloody fighting in the Pacific. We of course had no way of knowing that in a matter of weeks the Japanese would surrender too, ending a war that for the United States had begun on a Sunday morning almost four years before at Pearl Harbor. The fighting that might lay ahead of us was what we mostly talked about and thought about.

I never heard the expression "Double V for victory" (i.e., victory over the enemy overseas and victory over discrimination at home), either on the troopship or before, though I have been told that some blacks used it. We talked about our hatred for segregation and for the Japanese, but we never tied the two together that way.

President Roosevelt had just died in April of that year, and he received a lot of our attention during these bull sessions. As blacks, we admired Roosevelt because we felt his presidency had been good for us. We believed he had kept his promise to help turn things around for all black people; he had begun removing some forms of prejudice and discrimination, and we liked him for that. Mostly we felt that, in him, we had a friend in the White House, and when he died, it was as though we had lost a close relative. The man who had taken his place, President Truman, we had barely heard of.

In late June or early July we finally reached our destination, Okinawa, an island close to the Japanese homelands. After 100,000 Japanese and 12,000 American deaths, the island had come into total American control on June 21. When we arrived the combat troops were gone, and, except for a few Japanese snipers, Okinawa was in the backwater of the war. The results of battle were starkly evident. All the piers in the port had been knocked out, so our troopship had to anchor some distance from shore, and we were transferred to land by smaller landing craft. The sight we beheld was shocking. The hilly island of some 467 square miles had been leveled by naval shells, bombs, and artillery. The Japanese had dug themselves into the hillsides, and the Americans had tried to blow them out. The resulting damage was hard to believe. I still remember the scarred, desolate landscape, the caves in the hillsides, and the burial grounds everywhere I looked.

My unit, the 31st Quartermaster Battalion, was stationed in the center of the island near Naha, the capital. This city, too, was virtually leveled. Only here and there was a building still standing. The only clues we had to the thriving nature of the prewar city were the pavement and the remnants of masonry scattered everywhere.

We pitched our tents on the edge of Naha and set up what was to be my home for the year I spent on the island. We lived ten to a tent, in accommodations which were as good as might be expected under the conditions.

The battalion quickly began its rebuilding work. We constructed facilities for troops that were on the way. Okinawa was being readied as a supply center and embarkation point for other battles—even, it was rumored, for an invasion of Japan itself. I continued doing about the same thing I had been doing at Barclay: helping administer sick call. One new task was aiding the doctor in sanitation inspections. This job was important to keep down illness and disease among the tented troops. We never did any major surgery on the island because we did not have the facilities. We took care of all minor surgeries, but sent those needing more specialized help off the island to a larger hospital.

Though most of the injuries I saw were slight, I still learned a great deal about medicine during my year on the island. I got to watch the doctor as he performed minor surgery, and later I often assisted him. My most important lesson was learning how to deal with people, and how to ensure rapport between physician and patient. I began to acquire the skill of talking to a patient, extracting a history, and deciding whether an illness was physical or psychosomatic. Many times the doctor was absent on other duty, and we medics had to make the decisions on an individual's medical complaints. There were a lot of soldiers who were homesick and depressed and when they came in to complain about this pain or that we had to determine the root cause of the problem before we could help them. If the malady was the result of anxiety, we dealt with it differently than we did if the matter was strictly physical. I watched the doctor work, and sometimes I had to work alone. This experience helped me later when I had sole responsibility for my own patients.

I was fortunate too in working with the same fine, considerate white Jewish doctor I had worked with at Barclay. When I told him of my dream of going to medical school, he was most encouraging, and urged me to apply immediately, so I wrote to both Howard and Meharry. I jokingly thought to myself at that time that perhaps the fact I was fighting for my country might carry some weight with medical school officials if my grade point

53

average proved insufficient. I wonder even today whether the timely application, my grades, or my military studies was the key thing. Whatever it was, I received my acceptance while still on the island, and was able to enjoy my last few months on Okinawa confident that my dream was yet another step closer to reality.

Because we were in the backwater of the war, which was by then nearing its end, our battalion received very little attention from anyone. I personally had no relationship with the small Red Cross detachment on the island, but other blacks there and elsewhere did not have kind feelings toward the organization. We heard stories of discrimination and segregated blood, and we remained suspicious of the group's motives.

We had been on the island only a month or so when we learned about the dropping of the atomic bomb. Our reaction to the news was mixed. We did not want to have more Americans killed in further invasions, but there was something terrifying about a bomb that could kill that many people. None of the soldiers in my unit had anything good to say about the Japanese, yet we never considered the bomb as just retribution for the attack on Pearl Harbor and the loss of American lives in the war that followed. As soldiers, we hoped that this awful bomb might speed up the end of the war, but as black soldiers we wondered if it would have been dropped on the Japanese had they been a white nation like Germany or Italy.

The inhabitants of Okinawa were Orientals of mixed Chinese-Japanese ancestry, but it was difficult to know what they thought of the bomb or anything else. We had little contact with them. At first, those who were left on the island after the battle were terribly frightened. It took them a long time to deal with all the carnage and death they had seen. Slowly they recovered, and eventually many of those who had left returned to try to pick up the

54

pieces of their lives. They were uniformly friendly, but the language barrier and their shell-shocked condition prevented us from communicating very well. As time went on, however, conditions improved and soldiers and Okinawans became friendlier toward one another.

There were both black and white troops on the island, but the Okinawans seemed friendlier toward the blacks than toward the whites. I believe there were several reasons for this. For one thing, blacks were a curiosity. The Okinawans had never seen black people before, and they wanted to touch and feel our skins to be sure that we really were that color. At the same time, whites treated the Okinawans in the same way they treated us. They maintained a condescending posture of tolerance rather than acceptance toward both. I believe the Okinawans felt this attitude and drew closer to us as a result.

After living in the South and being repeatedly told that black was inferior, the white behavior did not surprise me. But to have a group of people *prefer* rather than despise me because of my skin color was a novel experience. I must say it felt good.

In looking back on my several years in the military, I still consider the time to have been well spent. My army years propelled me into medical school. They let me see a part of the world I would otherwise have never seen and to feel acceptance from others because of my race. This experience, plus the discovery of being able to compete successfully in an integrated situation, provided me with a hope and a pride no mere words could have produced. The army also taught me patience to accept limitations on our power to control our lives. In addition, it showed me the importance of going through proper channels to get things done. Finally, my military years hardened me—taught me that discipline is necessary to accomplish goals.

The army, then, taught me valuable lessons in race relations, personal conduct, and medical procedure. All these have stood me in good stead in subsequent years. But the army also showed me that, while there was indeed hope for me as a black man, the continued presence of military segregation and discrimination indicated the distance blacks still had to go. The army limited black soldiers to service units and provided little opportunity for us to advance past sergeant. Those of us who served in the war knew about Dorrie Miller's heroism at Pearl Harbor and about the black combat units on the ground and in the air. We cheered every one of their successes; we saw them as proving black capability on the battlefield. In our hearts we continued to hope that their valor and our faithful service would be rewarded in the postwar world, but the lack of opportunity to move ahead in the military was stifling, and I often thought of it and felt frustrated.

As the time drew near for me to leave Okinawa and return to civilian life, to my wife, and to my medical school career, I grew increasingly excited. A schedule of busy days had kept my loneliness to a minimum, but from time to time I had hoped for the day when Nita and I could get back together and have some semblance of real family life. My marrying her, even though we had to be separated almost immediately, had given me a sense of security I had never had before. Throughout our separation I kept reminding myself that some day we were going to have children and they would not have to suffer the trauma of a broken family as I had. Nita gave me, on the deepest personal level, what Alcorn had provided me more generally—a feeling of belonging. As I rode the troopship back to San Francisco, I looked forward to my medical career, but, even more, I anticipated the family life that I had been yearning for since my parents' divorce in 1932.

4
LEARNING MEDICINE

When I was mustered out of the army at Camp Shelby, Mississippi, in June 1946, I was close to Hattiesburg and so went home for a brief visit with my family. At that time my wife was in Starkville, a fairly long distance from the camp and Hattiesburg, and I was not able to see her immediately. I was enjoying my visit with my family when someone told me that the Chicago steel mills were hiring workers. The idea intrigued me. I needed money for my medical school expenses, and rumor had it that the pay in the steel mills was good, so I decided to go to Chicago to find a job for the summer. But first I went to Starkville to spend some time with Nita, the first time we had been together since our wedding over a year earlier.

The middle of June 1946 found me, fresh from the army, in South Chicago, where Nita joined me after her school year was finished. We lived in a small rental house about a ten-minute streetcar ride from the Carnegie Steel mill where I worked. The job was hard physical labor. I helped roll ore to the furnace to be smelted into steel. There was absolutely no thinking involved in the work; it was sheer muscular labor, quite a change from my recent army experience, but I didn't mind it. The pay was good, and I was happy about being with my wife and excited about the prospect of beginning medical school in the fall.

Mr. and Mrs. Douglas Conner in Chicago, 1946

The summer was a financial success. Nita was able to find a sales job in a clothing store near our house, and together we saved enough money to buy some clothes and build a sum large enough to pay my medical school entrance expenses. South Chicago was a rough place in those days, so after work we stayed close to home. Had we been more socially active, we would have been unable to save as much as we did. (I don't remember how much we saved, or how much I earned in the steel mills, but I remember being very pleased with both sums.)

When September arrived, I left the steel mills and took the train directly to Washington to begin my studies at

Howard University Medical School. Nita went back to Starkville to resume her job as a teacher in the Oktibbeha County Training School. That first year, while I was in medical school, she remained in Mississippi teaching and saving money for my school expenses.

I had passed the Howard University campus often while training at the Walter Reed Army Hospital, so it was not entirely strange to me when I arrived there in September 1946. The College of Medicine Building was situated along Georgia Avenue, and Freedmen's Hospital was located across the street and up the hill. I had seen both many times before. Still, it was exciting to realize that I would no longer be walking by these buildings and fervently hoping. Now I was going to go inside and fulfill my life's dream—to become a doctor.

The first several days were a blur of activity as I prepared to begin classes. My Chicago savings, when added to my veteran's benefits, provided me with enough money to pay the entrance fees and tuition. The following year I learned of a Mississippi scholarship and applied for it. The state scholarship board told me that I was eligible and that for every year after graduation that I practiced in the state the board would cancel one-fifth of the scholarship loan. I never received the full amount because of my veteran's benefits, but I did receive something like one hundred dollars a month, which enabled me to survive financially during my last three years of study. I was never able to get another summer job which paid me like the one in the steel mills, so the state money was crucial. I doubt whether I could have made it without these funds.

After paying my fees that first day, I began looking for a place to live and was fortunate to find a nice room with kitchen privileges near the campus. A lady lived in one part of the house, and rented the remainder to three medical students. I soon met my two housemates: Booker T.

Crumby, later a general practitioner in New Jersey, and Arthur Trent, who would become a general practitioner in Sacramento. The three of us quickly became friends and remained close throughout our medical training.

On the first day of classes we were given a tour of the facilities, and I was immediately struck by the quality of the staff. I was impressed to see so many Ph.D.'s and M.D.'s, almost all of whom were black; there were only a few white doctors on the faculty, and I remember working under them only in my third year, when we studied pediatrics.

My class of one hundred incoming freshmen was also predominantly black, but there were approximately four whites, five Chinese, five or six students from the Caribbean, and several from Africa. The Americans came from all over the country, though the largest bloc were Howard graduates. There seemed to be a quota system of two students from each state, though not every state was represented and some states had more than two. Anthony Jones and I were the two from Mississippi. Until his death in mid-1970s, Dr. Jones practiced in Holly Springs.

As we toured the school I experienced a strange feeling. I had dreamed of this moment all my life, yet now I felt frightened. I asked myself: "What have I gotten myself into? Can I make it?" My experience in the first class did not calm my anxieties. W. Montegue Cobb, a very dignified, impressive-looking man, was our anatomy instructor. As soon as we were seated, he looked around the room and announced: "Of all you people in the class, twenty will not be here at the end of the year. This course is so difficult that twenty of you will fail it." I was stunned, and so was everyone else in the room. We all began looking around, wondering whether we would be one of the doomed twenty. I thought to myself: what a terrible thing for an instructor to say. But as I think back on it, I realize that Dr. Cobb's statement did make us all determined not to fail. It stuck with me for the rest of my medical school career, and I have not forgotten it to this day.

As the shock of Dr. Cobb's matter-of-fact prophecy began to wear off, we were jolted again. We were taken for the first time into the anatomy laboratory. There we saw seventy cadavers—thirty-five bodies on dissecting tables on one side of the room, thirty-five bodies on dissecting tables on the other side of the room. I took one look, got one smell of the formaldehyde, and felt like turning around and walking out. The lab assistants did little to calm me. They told us we would have to dissect and identify every muscle, nerve, and bone in one of these bodies. If we did not fulfill these requirements correctly, we would fail the course. Again, the threat of failure was thrown in our faces. I wondered if my days in medicine were numbered.

That first semester I took courses in anatomy, biochemistry, and embryology. All the classes were conducted about the same way: there was an hour lecture followed by a two-hour laboratory. The course that most stands out in my memory is anatomy. We had an hour lecture and then spent two hours cutting into a human body. I had done some stitching of cuts before and had even assisted in surgery, but I had never done what I was being asked to do in that lab. I don't remember my first day on a cadaver, but I remember for a long time feeling very strange, very ticklish about cutting into a human body. Once I was fingering around very tentatively when one of the observing assistants came up to me. "Don't be so ginger about it," he said. "Get on with it. Cut out that muscle and identify it." Slowly I got used to it. After a while I could put in my two hours and go out and eat a sandwich without ill effect.

61

The first several months flew by in a whirl of classes, labs, and long hours of study. Sometimes it seemed as though I would never be able to get everything done. The biggest problem was memorizing countless medical terms so I could understand the lectures and the textbooks. After a while I learned to break down all the "ology" and "itis" words, and this made my task a little easier. We studied in groups, staying up late into the night banging information into each other's heads and grilling one another to make sure it stayed there. We kept up the pace all week, into and through the weekends. It was difficult, but I came to realize that if I studied and then studied some more I could make it. I began to have hope that I would not be one of the twenty flunkees that Dr. Cobb had spoken about that first day.

This hope that I *could* make it, and the sincere interest of most of the faculty kept me going. There were several instructors I particularly remember. Moses Wharton Young taught neuro-anatomy. He was a brilliant man, but he had a great deal of difficulty sharing his knowledge with his students. He always seemed to be talking over our heads; we had to work hard just to fathom his meaning. My favorite teacher was J. B. Johnson, our instructor in internal medicine and cardiology. He really knew his subject, and he never left the classroom until he was convinced that every student knew exactly what he had been talking about. Here was a man who really wanted me to get this stuff, I often thought, and I admired him for it.

The first two years of study followed about the same pattern; in short, we learned the theory of medicine. During our junior and senior years we did most of our work in Freedmen's Hospital, putting into practice what we had learned in the classroom. Reasoning and thinking replaced brute memorization, and I found this regimen much more to my liking. I got to work with patients and actually began to put my medical knowledge into practice. What I had learned at Alcorn had been very helpful during my first two years; now my army training and experience proved beneficial. I had done some of the things in the army that we were now being called upon to do. I found I had an advantage over some of my classmates. Many of them had not had the same practical experience.

Normally we were assigned a number of patients, so we could learn to communicate with them, document their medical histories, and do a physical examination. The first-year, second-year, and third-year residents checked over our work carefully, and once or twice a week the appropriate department head critiqued us. Throughout this process our supervisors placed great emphasis on our making the proper deductions from the facts at hand. We were taught differential diagnosis: decide what several things might be wrong with a patient and eliminate the possibilities one by one until the most logical illness is the only one left. We usually had to do our own lab tests because technicians put the requests of us lowly medical students far below those of physicians and residents.

Freedmen's Hospital did not provide the most up-to-date facilities, either for medical students or residents, or for that matter practicing physicians. It was a 500-bed facility that I thought had to have been built by the original freedmen. It looked that old. The equipment was not necessarily out of date, but it was hardly the most modern either. Our clientele was black and mostly from the lowest socioeconomic class. Blacks of means in Washington went to Gallinger Hospital; those who had difficulty paying for medical care came to Freedmen.

Though my hours during the junior and senior year of medical school remained long, I found I had more free time than I had had during the first two years and I was able to spend more time with my wife. Nita had remained in Starkville during my first year, but she joined me in June 1947. Her Aunt Sadye encouraged her to stay in Mississippi and continue making a living, but she was determined to take her chances in Washington. She decided that even if she had to scrub floors she would leave Starkville to be with me in Washington. She didn't have to scrub floors, but she did sell ice cream and milk for High's Dairy, a large Washington chain. After about a year of selling dairy products, she found a job as a salesperson/seamstress in a downtown Washington clothing store. It was wonderful having her with me, and the money she earned was very helpful.

My busy schedule kept our social life minimal, but once in a while we would board a bus and travel to one of the tourist attractions in the city. Washington was segregated, but it was not the total segregation found in the Deep South. When we went to a movie in downtown Washington, for example, we did not automatically find a Jim Crow balcony waiting for us. There was no mandatory segregated seating, though we did notice that blacks clustered in one area of seats and whites in another. Nita rarely experienced any prejudice in her work. Once in a while she would be rebuffed when she tried to serve someone, but normally there was no difficulty because the store's clientele was primarily upper middle class. There was segregated housing in the city, however, with sharply defined white and black areas, and blacks usually stayed in their own section and shopped in their own stores. For example, Nita and I spent most of our time in the black section surrounding Georgia Avenue.

We really didn't become involved in the day-to-day life of the city in general or the black area in particular. My studies kept me so busy that I was rarely ever able to go to church or participate in any community or university activities. I had little time for politics except to read about it in the newspapers. I didn't even try to visit any Mississippi congressman or senator because I thought it would be a waste of time, an exercise in futility. I saw no need to risk a racial snub just to see the inside of an unfriendly congressman's office. When Mississippi's delegation to the 1948 Democratic convention walked out and helped form the Dixiecrats rather than accept a civil rights plank, I knew things in my home state had not changed much during my absence.

My favorite political figure during my Howard years was Harry Truman. When President Roosevelt died and Truman became president, I wondered—like everybody else—what would happen to the country under his leadership. I said to myself: "This hillbilly from Missouri will do nothing but mess up." But I was in for a surprise. President Truman proved to be a man of his word. Whatever he believed in, he fought for. I liked this characteristic, especially when contrasted with FDR's desire to please everybody. A good example of Truman's attitude was his integration of the armed forces. He ignored all the flak he received and just did it. Perhaps the time had come anyway, but it still took Truman's determination to accomplish it. I liked Truman at the time, and I still admire him. I think he was one of the best presidents the United States has ever produced.

All in all, however, my thoughts were primarily on medicine, not on politics. My existence centered totally on my studies; my life was an uneventful routine. Work, work, work; study, study, study. It was only in the summers that I was able to do anything much different. After my first year I had to have an appendectomy, and spent the entire summer recovering. The next summer I got a job washing dishes and doing other menial work in the kitchen of Gallinger Hospital. The next two summers I worked in the data-processing unit of the Veterans Administration, having learned of the availability of the job from other medical students. It was not civil service work, but my veteran's status helped me get it anyway. I enjoyed the work because I learned how to use the then new data-processing equipment. The work was pleasant, the pay was good, and the activity was so different from my medical studies that I returned each fall refreshed and ready to tackle medicine again.

In the summer of 1947 I had to return home because of the death of my father. We had not seen much of each other since I left for Alcorn in 1939. As I have already mentioned, he and I had never had much of a relationship. He had rarely talked to me and had shown little or no interest in my activities. His drinking had always come before anything else. Despite our never being close, I felt that I had to go back for his funeral. I was fulfilling a duty by being there, but since he had never really been a part of my life, I could not very well feel any sense of loss at his death.

My medical training seemed to fly by, and soon I had to begin thinking about my future. I thought about becoming an obstetrician/gynecologist but decided instead to take an internship in general practice. The OB/GYN speciality would have required another three years of study, and I did not want to put Nita through another long period of waiting, particularly since she was then pregnant with our first child. The G.P. internship of one year seemed more manageable than the three years of OB/GYN at the pitiful amount of money that residents were being paid in those days.

Determining to go on a G.P. internship was only half the problem. The next question was where. During medical school the course work I took emphasized training doctors, not training black doctors. We did get extra instruction on hypertension and sickle cell anemia, common diseases among blacks, but that was about it—we were going to be doctors, not black doctors. Yet we could not escape the fact of our skin color. We would be black men with medical degrees going out to practice in a white-dominated and prejudiced world. There was little said about this unique fact of medical life in our classes, but when we had to make decisions about internship, this fact became obvious.

We had very little choice actually: there were only a handful of hospitals in the United States that accepted black interns. Some among the top 10 percent of the class might receive offers to become the first black interns at a prestigious white hospital, but the rest of us had to choose among black institutions like Harlem Hospital in New York, Provident Hospital in Chicago, the Homer G. Phillips Hospital in St. Louis, and a few others. There were no hospitals knocking at our door begging us to join their staffs. It was a disconcerting but unavoidable fact: society saw our black skins, not our sheepskins.

I could have gone to an internship in Harlem Hospital, but I decided on the Homer G. Phillips Hospital in St. Louis, primarily because I wanted to go South. (I never considered any Mississippi hospitals because I knew it would be fruitless to apply.) I also wanted to go to a place where I would get the type of experience that would help me in my later practice. At Freedmen's, the great number of residents limited the work of the interns. I believed that Phillips would be the kind of place where I could get a lot of experience. I was right: in that way, it turned out to be an intern's dream.

Homer G. Phillips, which was named after a prominent local black man, was a 500-bed hospital located in the middle of the black area in St. Louis. At that time St. Louis had two public hospitals: City Hospital No. 1—the white hospital, and City Hospital No. 2 (Homer G. Phillips)—

the black hospital. The entire staff was black and only rarely did a white doctor come to treat a patient. Though the staff was generally good, the facilities were not even as good as mediocre. In addition, the patient load was staggering. There were so many patients that adequate supervision of patients, nurses, and even interns like me was impossible. I often had mixed thoughts during my internship. On the one hand, the lack of supervision and the overabundance of patients meant I had enormous opportunities for any kind of medical experience I could imagine. On the other hand, I often wished I had more direct supervision to help me deal with the various medical problems I had to face. In looking back on the situation now, I believe I was forced to learn more than I would have learned under less hectic conditions. I believe I gained a great deal of valuable experience during my one year of internship. The medical care dispensed at Phillips was generally good.

I arrived at Phillips in June 1950 and left in July 1951. During that time, I had what was called a rotating internship. That is, I spent a month or two in the various departments within the hospital: two months on medicine, a month on pediatrics, and so on. I came into contact with medical problems of all different kinds. What supervision I had came from the first-year residents. They, in turn, were supervised by the second-year residents, who were under the third-year residents, who had to answer to the head of the department. I got to see the department head a few times a week if I was fortunate. Usually he was a practicing physician in the city, which meant he was available on a restricted basis. His private practice limited his time in the hospital, and this fact, perhaps more than any other, accounted for the freedom I experienced as an intern.

My year at Phillips was very demanding. I seemed to be on duty constantly. We twenty interns had to work every Friday afternoon all the way through to Sunday night. Of course, this time was in addition to our long hours during the week. There was no "TGIF" at Phillips; we all hated to see the weekends come. St. Louis in those days was a rough place, and the neighborhood surrounding the hospital was dangerous. Each weekend seemed to be a never-ending round of cut-ups and shoot-ups. I got the chance to do a great deal of sewing and fixing. Once it go so busy that I did an appendectomy with little or no supervision.

My most memorable experience happened one weekened when I was working in the emergency room. A big bruising man came walking in, huffing and puffing. There was an ice pick sticking out of his chest. He was really angry about the stabbing, but other than his anger and the heavy breathing, he was amazingly steady on his feet. He was rushed into surgery, and the surgeon found the pick had missed his heart by a hair. To this day I don't understand how that man was ever able to walk in on his own feet considering his condition.

As I hinted earlier, one of the hospital's major probjems was the fact that the department heads, the ultimate supervisors of interns, were practicing physicians. Most of them were good doctors, but some of them had very little concern about the hospital. They came in to see their patients and then rushed off to their practices as soon as they could. If an intern had this kind of a supervisor, he might just as well have had none at all. For this reason, I remain convinced that private-practice physicians should not be given the task of supervising interns in a hospital. The harried interns need all the help they can get, something busy private-practice physicians cannot provide.

Because of my busy schedule I had to live in a room provided by the hospital. Nita lived with her Aunt Sadye's sister, Louise Hunter, who was a St. Louis beautician. "Auntie," as we call Aunt Louise, would not hear of Nita living alone, not since she had an extra room in her house.

Since Nita gave birth to our first child in November 1950 and since I only made $25 a month, this living arrangement was financially most helpful to us. I could visit Nita and the baby only a couple of times during the week, so I was happy Auntie was there to help look out for them.

The birth of our daughter, Sadye Yvonne, at Homer Phillips was a major event in my life. I had routinely been going into the delivery room to help mothers deliver their babies, yet as I prepared to go in this time I could feel a difference, Now, it was my wife who was in labor, and I was the father of the child about to be born. Physician or not, I was still about to become a father for the first time, and I felt it. Perhaps I thought a bit too long. By the time I entered the delivery room, a third-year resident had already delivered the baby. I had missed the event; my wife's labor had been very short. In 1981 alone I delivered 178 babies; so I've seen more than my share of births, but I still wish I had made it into that room to witness the birth of my first daughter.

I had little time for any kind of social or religious activities during my year in St. Louis. I rarely even left the hospital. Still, I could sense something of the life in the city through the patients I saw. I could feel much more of a polarization of the races in St. Louis than I had in Washington. There was a stricter drawing of racial lines; there were stricter all-white and all-black communities. It was like the South of my youth, where the white and the black world rarely touched, but since I had little time to think about it and since I knew I would only be there for a year, I gave race relations in St. Louis little thought.

As my intern year drew to an end I began to think about establishing my practice. The only definite thoughts I had on the subject were not wanting to live in a big city and hoping to go back to Mississippi. I thought of Hattiesburg, Jackson, and Starkville. Since my childhood I had thought about the enormous need for black physicians in the state. My coming back would mean one more black doctor, and would bring hope to a few. My return would also fulfill the terms of my scholarship loan. I expected no one anywhere to make me any offers. I knew I would have to go out and find a suitable place myself. Considering that my goal was Mississippi and considering the 1950s racial climate in the state, I was not sure what community would accept me.

I did not worry very much about finding a place to establish my practice because I was confident something would work out. As my internship drew to an end, my excitement about finally reaching my medical goal was the predominant thought in my mind. As long as I could remember I had dreamed about being a physician in a black community, healing hurts and making life better for a suffering people. I was on the verge of beginning that effort. It was hard to believe, and it was exhilarating, all at the same time. Dr. Douglas L. Conner, M.D., was about to hang out his shingle.

5

STARKVILLE PHYSICIAN

Near the end of my internship a series of events determined where I was to practice medicine all my professional career. I had decided I wanted to return to Mississippi after leaving the Homer G. Phillips Hospital, and a Mississippi town let me know plainly that it wanted my services.

Until Nita and I married, I had not known any of her family. The day of our wedding I had met Sadye Wier, the aunt who raised her, but I had not met Aunt Sadye's husband, Robert. Uncle Rob was a barber in Starkville and a leader of the black community there. He was a quiet, dignified man of few words but great integrity and solid common sense. I first met him when I came to Starkville in 1946 to see Nita after my return from Okinawa. Uncle Rob and I hit it off at the time, but we had little contact after that because of my busy medical school and internship schedule. However, as I would later learn, Uncle Rob remembered me as more than the husband of the niece he had helped raise; he saw me as the physician he, Aunt Sadye, and other black Starkville leaders had long dreamed the town should have.

One day while I was visiting Nita and our baby Sadye Yvonne, Aunt Sadye's sister, Louise Hunter, told me she had just heard from Uncle Rob. He had helped form a committee which wanted me to visit Starkville at their expense to consider the town for my future practice. I knew Nita would be happy to return to Starkville, but I knew little about the place other than what she had told me. At any rate, I decided to go look around. Nita said little. She never pressured me in any way, and neither did Uncle Rob nor Aunt Sadye. I was left completely free to make my own decision.

In May 1951 I took the train from St. Louis and spent a weekend in Starkville. I was given a tour of the town and the neighboring Mississippi A and M College (now Mississippi State University). The black committee carefully told me that they had checked out the possibility of my coming with the town's white leadership, and that the response of the whites was favorable. White doctors had also promised their cooperation, which meant I would receive immediate hospital privileges. When Uncle Rob took me to meet various white leaders in the community, they repeated their support. Everyone—the mayor, businessmen, physicians, and ordinary black and white citizens—extended a welcome. Though I did not tell anyone, I made up my mind right then. The fact that both blacks and whites seemed to want me was reason enough for me to come. I also began to think that my alternatives were not as attractive; Jackson was just too big, and if I went back to Hattiesburg it would be a while before people who had known me as a child could accept me as a physician.

So, as the committee in Starkville, consisting of people like shoe-shine parlor owner George Evans, undertaker B. L. Robinson, shoe shop owner Ernest Jones, barber Fred Gandy, Uncle Rob, and others, took me around, I made my decision. I would accept their offer.

In 1951 Starkville was a small town in the hill country of northeast Mississippi with a population of just over 7,000 of which about 30 percent was black. The area called itself "the Dairy Center of the South," and the presence of the Borden Milk Company plant attested to the volume of milk produced there. In addition, Starkville was the seat of one of the state's major institutions of higher learning, the then all-white Mississippi A and M.

The city's hub was the downtown area along Main Street. Here were located the Oktibbeha County courthouse, the movie theater, and all the major stores. Nearby were the Borden plant, the white Baptist and Methodist churches, and city hall. West of downtown was Greensboro Street, the most prestigious residential street in town, the area where the leading white families lived. Gillespie Street, upper Washington Street, Curry Street, Long Street, and Henderson Street were the major black streets in town. Cow pastures existed where today stand major residential areas and businesses. Starkville was a pleasant country town with a thriving business district and, as a bonus, a state college.

As I was being driven around town, I liked what I saw. As a black man, however, there were several things that bothered me. I noticed how careful black leaders were to gain the prior approval of whites for everything they did. My visit was merely the most conspicuous example of this fact. I noted, too, that although all the white leaders I met were pleasant, there was an undercurrent of paternalism in their attitude toward me and the black sponsors who were introducing me. I must say, however, that I did not think about the racial situation very much. I had grown up in the South and had experienced such treatment and the even harsher open prejudice all my life. I mentally shrugged my shoulders and concentrated on the positive aspects of the locality.

I particularly liked the four white physicians who made up the Starkville medical profession of that day: Charles Dodd, John Feddy Eckford, Felix Long, and Hunter

Scales. Since I would have closer contacts with them than with any other residents, I was happy when they all expressed a hearty welcome and urged me to come.

I quickly discovered that, though the four men formed a very small medical community, there was some friendly competition among them. Dr. Long and Dr. Eckford had competing hospitals: Dr. Long's had forty beds; Dr. Eckford's about eight. The black committee had made arrangements for me to have hospital privileges at Dr. Long's hospital. Consequently, my tour there was the more important part of my visit.

During my stays at Freedmen's Hospital and at Homer G. Phillips, I had recognized the equipment inadequacies of both places. Yet I would soon find that the Felix Long Hospital in Starkville was even more poorly equipped than those two facilities. I knew from the beginning that I would not have the advantages of the latest medical technology if I came to Starkville, but I rationalized that I could live with the situation.

The hospital itself was, of course, segregated. Today the building is the integrated Community Counseling Center. The Oktibbeha County Hospital, a modern 100-bed facility, has long since replaced it as the area's main medical facility. Walking into the old hospital, one entered a hallway between two rooms: the room on the right was the black waiting room, the one on the left the waiting room for whites. The hallway proceeded past these rooms and led to two wings: the wing to the right housed the black patients, the wing to the left the white patients. There were approximately twenty beds on each side, though the white side had semiprivate rooms with baths while the black side had rooms with three or four beds and no private baths. The operating room, the delivery room, and the emergency room were used in common, and both black and white wings had white nurses and black nurses aides. The quality of care seemed to be the same on both sides, and I was of course pleased with that, if not with the segregation.

My next concern was finding a place to establish my office. (Uncle Rob and Aunt Sadye offered Nita and me the use of a large bedroom in their house, so I was not concerned about finding living accommodations.) One of the members of the black committee, Fred Gandy, offered me the use of the second floor in a building he had recently built on Washington Street about a block north of Main Street and two to three blocks northeast of the hospital. This building had been roughly built from surplus lumber, and it needed a good deal of work, but it was the best available site. When the committee of black leaders offered to pay my first six months' rent there, that settled the issue. I determined to establish my practice in Fred Gandy's building.

When my visit was over and I boarded the train to return to St. Louis, I did it with a feeling of relief. I had found a place for my practice. Within a week Nita and I called Uncle Rob and told him of our decision. We planned to come to Starkville as soon as my internship was over.

When we arrived in July, I immediately began work on my office. The second floor of the building was unfinished—rough wood floor and walls. I attached sheet rock to the walls and put down linoleum floors. I was not pleased with the stairway leading up to the second floor, so I spent time making it safer. When I was finished, the second floor had three rooms: a waiting room which could hold about fifteen people, a small office, and a treatment room. I had heard of an older doctor retiring from his practice in Okolona, Mississippi, so I drove there and purchased his equipment.

I saw a few patients in late July, but I did not officially

begin my practice until August 6. I placed an ad in the local paper announcing my presence as the town's new "colored physician." The paper also ran a small story telling of my background and training. Now it was a matter of opening the doors to see if any patients would come.

I well remember that first day. When I left the Wier house that morning, my family was all excited. I arrived at my bright new office, its floors and walls gleaming, its used furniture freshly polished. I wore a white coat and I had my nurse, Roxie Mobley, all decked out in white too. There we stood waiting for the first patient to arrive. That first day I saw a grand total of three people. All that first week, it was equally slow. Little by little, however, patients came in and then passed the word to others. Over a period of time, my practice grew.

I also began my work at the Felix Long Hospital. I do not remember my first days there, though I do retain some overall impressions. The white doctors were true to their word and welcomed me to the staff. The white nurses at first saw me as an object of curiosity, but by and large they treated me well too. Of course, in any situation there will always be some prejudiced people, so I did have some minor difficulties. A few nurses showed their disdain for me by their slowness in following the orders I wrote up or by giving me one of those looks which indicated: "Who are *you* to be telling me what to do?" I quickly learned how to deal with these few: I was overly kind to them. They had no choice but to temper their racism. They were not first-class nurses anyway, so their discriminatory attitude only added to their other limitations. To most of the nurses, however, my race did not seem to matter one way or another.

I was not the only black in the hospital. There were black nurses aides, janitors, and kitchen help, and they were uniformly friendly and helpful. They freely gave me the kind of advice blacks normally give each other in any new situation: "Go slow; take it easy; be careful." I received no warnings about any particular individuals or about any racial etiquette. I received general advice from people whose pride in my being there was mingled with a sense of protection. I could see they related to me, a black man, in a way they were not able to relate to the white doctors.

Most of my time was spent treating patients in my office. Each week my practice grew larger as more and more of the area's blacks learned of my presence and received assurances that I was competent. Being a black professional in a black community is never easy. White society has a tendency to lump blacks together and ascribe a unity, a oneness, that is simply not there. Blacks do not automatically support someone because he or she is black. In fact, blacks will often support a white person simply because he or she is white.

When I first came to Starkville, I received my strongest support from rural blacks rather than from blacks in town. Even today, most of my patients are from rural areas. Before I came, some of these had gone to Dr. Thomas L. Zuber, a black physician in West Point, or to Dr. H. Charles Hunter, who practiced in Columbus. Starkville blacks had been going to the white doctors in town.

To this day, among a segment of the black community, especially among the middle class, there is an attitude that if something is done by a white person it is done better. I believe this is a carry-over from the days of slavery and later discrimination. Blacks have long been told that white is superior and black is inferior. All our lives we have been told in countless ways that we are nobody. This attitude rubs off, and some of us have adopted it as our own.

There is a joke in the black community that expresses this attitude well. Two people are selling ice at an identical price; one a white man, the other a black man. They both bring their ice into a black neighborhood. The white man sells all his ice; the black man sells none. When asked why they have patronized the white iceman and not the black one, the black buyers respond: "The white man's ice is colder."

I have often had to deal with this kind of attitude toward my own practice and toward the activities of other black professionals and businessmen. I always attack such attitudes head-on. I tell people who have such feelings: "Think of your children. You might have a child who wants to become a dentist, or a doctor, or a teacher. If you have this kind of attitude, you give that child a complex; you make him or her feel that there is no need to try because blacks can't measure up." In other words, if blacks do not support black professionals and black businessmen, nobody will. Without black support, blacks as a group will never develop a base for black progress.

When I began my practice, most of my patients were of the lowest socioeconomic class and were very down-to-earth. They were most appreciative of my services; they did what I told them to do without question. Most of them did not have much money, and at times they could not afford my $3 office visit fee, yet they did not want to receive treatment for nothing. Some would bring in corn, potatoes, peas, peanuts, or chickens—not to reimburse me, but as a way of saying, "Take this until I have the money to pay you." At first I had nothing but black patients. Then I began getting a few white patients—men suffering from venereal disease who came to see me so that the white doctors would not know of their affliction.

Today my patients are much more varied and sophisticated. Ninety-five percent of them are black, but there is a much greater mixture of social classes and city residents as well as inhabitants of the county. As a group they are much more willing to ask questions about their treatment, what the side effects of medication might be, and so forth. I'm happy to see this attitude, and I encourage it. I want my patients to know as much as they can about their own bodies.

Rarely today do I receive payment in the form of farm goods. Most of my patients are now able to pay the $15 office visit fee I charge. My white patients are also a more varied group. In an average week I see three or four white patients for the same variety of diseases and problems I see my black patients. Most of these whites come from the lower socioeconomic class.

When I first began practicing, I was only thirty-one, and a young looking thirty-one at that. This caused some concern, particularly among my older patients. Some would come in and bluntly ask, "Boy, are you sure you know what you're doing? Just where did you say you went to school?" Others would deal with these same anxieties by joking about the fact that on the first floor, next to Fred Gandy's barbershop, there was a black undertaker's office. Some patients would laughingly warn me, "Now you be sure I don't end up going downstairs."

I learned very quickly that one of my best allies in overcoming black concern about my age and competence was Dr. Hunter Scales, one of the town's four white doctors. I had a great deal of respect for Dr. Scales as a person. He was one of the most forthright people I have ever known. He told people exactly what he thought, sometimes in language of the saltiest kind. In his own practice, whether a black or a white patient came in, he or she signed a common office log, to be treated, not according to race, but according to place on this list. Once in a while a white patient would complain about having to be served after a black patient. Dr. Scales had a simple answer: "If you don't like it, get the hell out of here." Another time, a

80

patient told Dr. Scales about a quack remedy for his sore back. Dr. Scales disdainfully retorted: "You might as well have backed up to a mule and let him kick the hell out of you."

Unbeknownst to me, Dr. Scales was praising me in his own inimitable style and helping wipe away black doubts about my competence. Any number of blacks told me: "I went to Dr. Scales, and he said you were one of the best damned doctors in town, and I should start coming to see you." Dr. Scales never told me he was doing this, but in his own way he was helping me get established.

I really worked hard in those early years. Each day I began around 7 or 8 A.M. with my hospital rounds and, except for an hour off for dinner and another for supper, I worked until 10 or 11 P.M., Monday through Saturday. After a number of years at this pace, I began to close the office around 5 or 6 P.M. Later I took half a day off on Wednesday, and then all day. Some years ago I began going in on Wednesday and taking Saturday off. Sometimes, though, I still go in on Saturdays when I have four or five patients to see. I may end up staying four or five hours, because other patients come in when they see the door open. In the late 1970s I went to Macon in nearby Noxubee County every Saturday to provide basic medical care in a trailer clinic established by several Macon black leaders. In 1982–84, until a resident physician moved there, I spent two Saturdays a month in a little town called Shuqualak, providing basic medical care in a federally funded program.

The first three years or so in my practice I also made a lot of house calls. Some would take me as far away as fifteen to twenty miles into the county. I would spend two to three hours going and coming to see one patient. As my practice grew, I stopped doing this because it was not the most efficient use of my time. In most cases the person I went to visit was fully capable of coming into the office. I can, in fact, remember only one unusual house-call case. I had a patient in a rural area who had had a stroke that had paralyzed one side of his body: his arm, leg, and the muscles of mastication. I wanted to admit him into the hospital, but he and his family would not hear of it, and I reluctantly agreed to work with him at home. I inserted a tube so that he could receive nourishment, and I trained his family to care for him. I regularly went to check on him and change the tube. I ministered to him in this way for seven months. But this was an unusual case. Most of my house-call patients could come in to see me in my office, and the end of house visits caused no real hardships and increased my ability to treat a larger number of patients.

In addition to treating my own patients, I have helped other physicians when they were out of town or unable, for any other reason, to take care of their own patients. I have also taken my turn "on call" at the hospital. At one time this created problems. Some whites simply would not think of receiving treatment from a black doctor. Consequently, whenever I was on call, there would always have to be a back-up white physician in case someone refused my services. Usually the nurses handled the whole matter. They could size up a patient pretty well and decide: "Now, here's someone who won't want Dr. Conner to treat him." Then, they'd call me and explain the situation. But, even with their care, I would sometimes drive to the hospital only to be told by a sick or injured individual: "You're colored; I don't want you to treat me." When that happened I never expressed any anger. I said: "Okay, we'll just call another doctor." Then I left quietly and forgot it.

I never have to face the situation now. The county hospital has a policy that a patient may refuse treatment from a physician on call only if he or she prefers to be treated by his/her own physician. Otherwise, treatment will be rendered by the physician on call or not at all.

In the early years various physicians covered for me when I had to be away, and I reciprocated the favor. Again, a white physician had to be available to take care of any white patient who refused my services. In recent years I have had an agreement with two other solo practicing white physicians in town. Normally, only one or the other is out of town at one time, so I end up taking care of the absent physician's black patients while the other white physician takes care of the absent doctor's white patients.

And so, I maintained a busy schedule in the early years of my practice. I was pleased with everything about it except that I had a second-floor office. Some of my patients found it difficult to climb the stairs. I began to think of finding a better location. A black farmer named Joe Lindsay owned a café just two buildings north of my office, and as his way of helping me in my medical practice offered to sell me his building for $8,000, at $150 per month without down payment or interest. I jumped at the chance. I remodeled the café, including scraping splattered grease from the walls, and moved my office there. I am still practicing at that same location today.

Whether I was on call or in the hospital or moving my office, my life revolved around my medical career. I attended the Second Baptist Church, but I joined no social clubs and I cultivated very few friends. I was closest to Uncle Rob Wier, who was like a father to me. I depended a great deal on his calm, sound advice. I made no big decision without consulting him. He and Aunt Sadye taught me how to drive a car, and he even co-signed my first car note. During the two years Nita and I lived in the Wier house, he and I spent a lot of time just talking. He was a sharp businessman and a caring individual. He helped fill a void my father had created in my life.

The 1950s were also the years when Nita and I were establishing our family. Sadye Yvonne had been born in St. Louis in 1950, and our second daughter, Eileen Yvette, was born in Starkville in 1954. In 1956 we adopted a twelve-year-old boy named Richard Holmes whom I will discuss more fully in later pages. Yvette did not come as quickly as Sadye Yvonne had, so this time I was able to be present at the delivery. Yvette was a large baby, and Dr. Long had difficulty delivering one of her shoulders. As a result, she developed temporary paralysis and we had to take her to a specialist in Memphis for three months, during which time she had to wear a brace. Fortunately she has suffered no complications from this condition.

In 1953 we moved from the Wier residence, where we had lived since 1951, to our own house on Gillespie Street. The property that we bought was mainly a hollow with water and frogs, but we had it filled in and had a black contractor, Rufus Nicks, build a house according to plans we had worked out during the previous year. It was a great day when we occupied our own home. The years of struggle and hard work had been rewarded. My family had a home in which to grow and prosper.

However, I have never spent as much time with my family as I wish I had—my practice has always kept me too busy. In the early years I worked until 10 or 11 o'clock every evening, and this left me little time for Nita and the children except on Sundays. The first several years we owned our own home we had a regular New Year's Day reception, but as my practice grew this too went by the wayside. My wife taught at Bankhead School in Noxubee County from 1955 to 1961, and this situation also made social life difficult. (A teaching position in Starkville did not open up until 1964.) During most of the year we did family things only on a hit-and-miss basis, usually in conjunction with some school activity. It was only in the summers that we spent any appreciable time together. Each year I attended the meeting of the National Medical Association in places like Chicago, Los Angeles, and New York, and I took the entire family with me. After I attended the medical sessions, we spent several weeks vacationing together. In this way I could give my family my undivided attention for a large block of time. I could also give them the advantages of travel.

I believe my family benefited from being "Dr. Conner's family"; doors were open to them that were not open to other blacks in the community. Yet I also know it was difficult to have a physician for a husband and father. The children never said to me, "Daddy, why aren't you home more?" though they might have said it to their mother. There is no question in my mind that Nita is responsible for holding us together as a family. She has had to sacrifice a great deal, taking on the responsibility of rearing the children oftentimes by herself. She has frequently told me how much she wished I could spend more time with her and the family, yet she never pushed too hard; she was always supportive. She is an unusual woman to have put up with all she has over the years. Were I to do it again, I would spend less time with my practice and more time with my family. I am always pleased to see younger doctors setting aside time to keep their family and medical responsibilities in perspective. I wish I had been that far-seeing.

I don't want to give the impression that having a physician for a father is all bad. As soon as my children were old enough, I took them to the office and taught them how to take blood pressures, pulse rates, and temperatures, and do simple laboratory procedures. I never demanded that they become interested in medicine; I simply exposed them to it. Evidently it had some effect because all three of my children are medical professionals. Sadye is a graduate of

Meharry Medical School and a practicing pediatrician in Los Angeles. Yvette is a registered nurse in Nashville. Richard Holmes graduated from Michigan State University Medical School and is a physician in Birmingham, specializing in emergency room medicine.

Whether my children went into medicine solely because of my example is, of course, problematical. However, all my medical career I have been aware of the influence I might be having on black youngsters. I often recall how Dr. Charles Smith had been my role model simply by being there as I walked to school in Hattiesburg. As I work on my lawn, I think of the impression his lawn and house had on me. Deep down, I think I am following in Dr. Smith's footsteps.

As I conduct my practice I have these same feelings. Whenever I see a black youngster express interest in medicine, I try to encourage him with odd jobs in my office. I am particularly moved when I see a youngster who is down-and-out because it reminds me of my own youth. I reach out to such a person and try to motivate him. I tell him that he is capable of better, that he has to break the crutch of using blackness as an excuse for standing still, doing nothing, and depending on charity. I suppose I will never know how successful I've been in these efforts, just as Dr. Smith never really knew of the tremendous influence he had on me.

6
MEDICAL REFLECTIONS

I kept no count of the patients I treated over the years, but if I had, the number would be a large one. In 1981 alone I delivered 178 of the 680 babies born at the county hospital. Each day I see thirty to forty patients in my office and visit others who are in the hospital.

I try to treat each patient carefully and with dignity, recognizing that I am no better than any one of them simply because of my medical training. I always try to remember that I have strengths and weaknesses like everyone else. When I first began my practice, I was fresh out of internship and had limited experience in dealing with patients on my own. At the same time, my education had been good, so my knowledge of medicine was strong. As time has passed, I have gained more than thirty years of experience, and now I think my greatest strength is my ability as a diagnostician. I believe I have mastered the fine line of knowing when to treat a patient and when to send him or her to a specialist. On the other hand, I wish I had more time for postgraduate education. I regularly go to medical meetings; I participate in the monthly in-service training at our hospital; I listen carefully to the representatives of the drug companies; and I read the medical journals that come across my desk. But I wish I could do more. I think I keep up, but I am not satisfied that I have done enough in this area.

During the last thirty-four years I have had moments of great satisfaction and moments of sadness in my practice. There are two incidents which I might call my greatest disappointment and also my greatest satisfaction as a physician.

During the early years of my practice I regularly delivered babies in my office to try to keep expenses for my financially struggling patients to a minimum. One of these was a woman who had a fairly uncomplicated delivery but who suddenly began bleeding profusely. I knew I had to get her to the hospital and immediately had an ambulance called while I tended to her. I rushed her to the emergency room, but she died ten or fifteen minutes after arrival. I was distraught. I kept wondering whether she would have lived had she delivered at the hospital where I would have been able to work more efficiently to stop the bleeding and begin blood transfusions. To this day, I don't know the answer to the question. But she was the last woman I delivered in my office. From that time on I have delivered only in the hospital.

My greatest satisfaction also resulted from childbirth. It was about 1957, when I was still delivering children in my office. A child was born with an omphalocoele—the liver, intestine, stomach, and so forth all hanging out. I immediately called Dr. Dempsey Strange, who had recently become the town's only surgeon. He took one look and agreed with my diagnosis. We immediately took the baby to the hospital, and I assisted Dr. Strange as he did temporary surgical repair so that we could send the baby to specialists at the University Medical Center in Jackson. There she had several more operations. In 1981 this woman gave birth to her own child. With the help of Dr. Mike Howe, a local gynecologist, I delivered her baby by caesarean section. It was an exciting moment as I realized what I had been a part of: a woman who might very well have died without swift medical care twenty-five years previously was now herself producing life. It was an experience I will never forget.

Most physicians have an experience like this only on rare occasions. Much of the time our work is far less dramatic. Yet over the years those of us in the medical profession have participated in a truly spectacular drama: the incredible progress of our science. So many of the things we as physicians routinely do today—and 90 percent of the drugs I now routinely prescribe every day—were not even in existence when I began my practice in 1951. Most significant of all has been the availability of numerous antibiotics to treat a wide range of pathogenic microorganisms. The phenomenal new technology, which allows procedures like cardiac catherization, dialysis for kidney failure, and vastly improved surgical techniques, is the other major innovation in my lifetime for the everyday treatment of illness and disease. The availability of antibiotics has vastly decreased the incidence of infection complications in all kinds of medical situations. Dialysis has extended life expectancy for kidney patients from a matter of weeks or at best months to years. All the various medical advances that are available to patients at the most local level have resulted in saving lives which in the pre-World War II period would surely have been lost.

When most people think of medical advances, they usually think of doctors in large urban medical centers portrayed on television and in the movies. I have been a small-town physician all my professional career, yet I have experienced these changes myself. There simply is no comparison between the Starkville medical situation now and what it was in 1951 when I arrived. The quality of medical care has improved a thousandfold. When I came, we were still in the horse-and buggy age; today we are as modern as any community our size can be expected to be. The big difference is the existence of our modern 100-bed hospital and the presence of specialists. I believe firmly that first-class medical care is impossible without the availability of specialists. I have never done much surgery, but when I came to Starkville Dr. Eckford and Dr. Long had to do a great deal of it because there was no surgeon available. Dr. Strange arrived on the scene soon after I did, and he made an enormous difference, Today, Starkville has four surgeons, two pediatricians, one orthopedic surgeon, two internists, an opthalmologist, a urologist, three gynecologists of whom two are obstetricians, and a psychiatrist, in addition to a large number of family specialists and general practitioners. We still need a neuro-surgeon, a cardiologist, and another psychiatrist, and we could use many more primary-care practitioners. But, all in all, medical treatment in Starkville has progressed light years in the time I have practiced there. We are in better shape than other towns of our size, though, of course, we cannot compete with the larger urban areas in the state or nation.

Over the years I have also noticed a difference in the physicians serving the Starkville community. Since 1975 there has been a large influx of general and specialist physicians. They are mostly young, hardworking, talented, and dedicated. They have improved on the fine medical care we earlier doctors tried to provide. They also have more liberal attitudes on race. When I first came to Starkville the white physicians welcomed me, but it took about five years for them to accept me as an equal. They were products of Mississippi segregation, and I was, after all, a black man. Though I was fresh from medical school and my internship, they never asked my opinion on any medical matters. Today the new young doctors do not have their predecessors' baggage of segregation. Race no longer plays a role in Starkville medical relationships.

In the old days segregation was a fact of life at all echelons of southern medicine. Black medical professionals were not allowed to practice in many hospitals and were excluded from professional organizations. In Mississippi, black doctors were not allowed to join the Mississippi Medical Association, which is affiliated with the American Medical Association, and thus we were automatically barred from national AMA membership. As a result, black doctors founded the National Medical Association and established a state affiliate, the Mississippi Medical and Surgical Association. In my area of the state we also founded the North Mississippi Medical, Dental, and Pharmaceutical Association and met every three months to maintain professional ties and keep on top of the latest scientific findings. This regional group disbanded in the late 1970s when the problem of black medical professionals participating in local hospitals lessened. However, the Mississippi Medical and Surgical Association maintains its existence, as does its parent National Medical Association. The Mississippi Medical Association has called for merger several times, but we black doctors continue to hold back. We worry that medical society integration would resemble that of so many other groups—blacks would be shunted aside. With our own group, we can deal with problems of special concern to the black community—for example, the need for more black physicians. We have our own forum to express black medical needs, and we use it regularly to let the state power structure know our concerns.

I know that the AMA does not practice discrimination any longer, but I still have bad feelings toward it because of past practices. I am also opposed to what I consider the antipublic attitude of the organization. Everything the

AMA does seems to be geared to keeping doctors on a pedestal, to maintaining them as a super-elite. The AMA Political Action Committee is highly organized and well financed. It seems to try to influence congressmen to support legislation to advance the well-being of doctors rather than concentrating on improving health care for the public at large.

On the other hand, I believe the AMA has a definite role to play in American life. The AMA, in conjunction with the NMA, should take as its primary task the identification of national health-care needs and present its recommendations in a positive way to Congress and the national administration. As it stands now, the AMA reacts rather than leads. It presents a negative voice rather than a positive one. Physicians have important things to say about the nation's medical needs, and the AMA ought to be the voice articulating these recommendations. The federal government has already taken action and will continue to take action on the medical front whether or not we physicians state our opinions.

The federal government today plays a major role in the nation's medical system as a result of the passage of the Medicare/Medicaid laws. When Lyndon Johnson fought to have these programs passed, the NMA was a major supporter of his efforts. I personally supported LBJ too. I saw the need for programs such as these; I saw too many poor people, white as well as black, being denied medical care because of their inability to afford it. Yet over the years I have not been happy with the direction of these programs. Medicare/Medicaid has been instrumental in causing the skyrocketing rise in medical costs. Unfortunately too many hospitals and too many physicians have viewed the programs as a way to ensure a secure flow of funds; they have abused them. There is temptation to increase the flow of federal funds into a hospital by raising rates. Our hospital, which receives 50 percent of its generated income from the federal government, does not do this, but I suspect some hospitals do. The result is ever rising medical costs.

At the same time, something has to be done to help poor people afford necessary medical care. Some people argue that the answer is National Health Insurance. I believe the intent of such a program is good because it would provide for people who cannot afford medical treatment on their own. By the same token, however, it would also fuel the rising costs of medical treatment even more.

I believe that the federal government has a definite role to play in the nation's medical-care system. I am not one of those who call for government to pull out of this and every other area. If that happened, I am convinced that poor people would suffer terribly. But I believe there is a better way for the government to play its role. First of all, there is a real need for a reform of the Medicare/Medicaid program. The government should crack down hard on the Medicare/Medicaid mills which unfortunately exist all over the country. Those who really need help ought to get it; those who are cheating the government—whether physicians, hospitals, or patients—ought to be stopped and punished.

Next, I think a new system ought to be established. Everyone should have some sort of health insurance, but it should not be solely a federal government responsibility. There should be a partnership between government, private industry, and patient, each paying a fair share of the patient's medical expenses. The patient's share of the cost should be based on his/her ability to pay, but each person should pay something. This share of the cost, I believe, would help prevent patient abuse and, more important, would give each person a sense of personal responsibility for his/her own care. I cannot say that such a plan would be a panacea for the nation's health-care problems, but I believe it would be an improvement over the present system.

Another area of medical care that I feel strongly about is the matter of where and how people are treated. I am convinced that health care for the affluent and for the less affluent must be provided in the same facility. If the poor are treated in one facility and the affluent in another, the facility for the poor quickly becomes overcrowded. It also becomes a vehicle for training new physicians who, upon being trained, move to a less crowded, better equipped facility for the affluent. No matter what kind of medical system, no matter what kind of health-insurance program, all patients must be treated in the same facility, regardless of their economic situation, or there is no equal medical treatment for all.

As a physician, I am of course aware of the public perception that doctors are greedy and interested not in their patients but in their patients' wallets. The public blames physicians for the skyrocketing medical costs. It galls me when I hear talk like this. For example, I have only raised my own office visit fee in thirty-odd years from $3 to $15. My fees have not even kept pace with inflation over this period. Certainly some doctors charge more than I do, but they may have higher expenses or they are specialists. If anything, many doctors are not business-minded enough in handling their finances. Over the years I have been much too lax in handling the financial side of my practice. I have always taken every patient, treated him or her, and in effect said: "Here is my bill. If you pay it, okay; if you don't, okay." I have learned over the years that too many people are all too ready to take advantage of a generous physician, and I have tightened my bill collecting, but I am still not as efficient as I ought to be. I have lost a good bit of income because of my unwillingness to press for the payment of all my outstanding bills.

I am convinced that the great majority of physicians do not stay in the medical profession in order to make a lot of money. If money were the primary consideration, most doctors would have entered other professions where the money is better and where they would not have to put up with the long hours, the inconvenience, and all the other frustrations of medicine. It is true that physicians make a comfortable living, but few become very wealthy unless they have an outside income. Physicians, like others, are entitled to a reasonable compensation. The years of study and the long hours of hard work entitle them to this consideration. I recognize that there are physicians, as there are people in any profession, who give the rest of us a bad name because of their attitude toward money or because of their incompetence. I also recognize that the medical profession has done a poor job of policing itself. We tend to cover up unless there is grossly abnormal behavior. Yet the existence of the relative few is not justification for condemning the many. Most doctors are dedicated professionals who deserve public respect and support.

I can of course understand why some people have the perception of physicians they have. There are some doctors who seem more concerned about the money they can make and the life-style they can maintain than the service they can provide to people. There are those who aspire to be among the leading twenty in the community. Such status takes money, so they overcharge and sometimes do unnecessary procedures to keep the money rolling in and thus their life-styles secure.

The increasing number of lawsuits has also caused the cost of medical care to rise. In my own case, I try to keep expenses down for my patients, but I find myself ordering ever more tests to protect myself in case of a suit. A lawyer gets to a patient—even one a doctor has treated for years—and points out that this or that should have been done. Suddenly the doctor is in court. I have been threatened with legal action on three or four occasions, but fortunately nothing came of it. Usually a caring doctor is not sued as quickly as the smart aleck. But, unfortunately, concern for a patient is no protection against a suit.

Despite my respect for the majority of practicing physicians, I still believe there is need for improvement in our profession. For example, we need to make medical care much more of a team responsibility. Physicians need to work in concert, not only with specialists but also with respiratory therapists, social workers, nutritionists, and other health professionals to provide the best possible treatment in each case. In my years of practice, I would estimate that only 25 percent of the patients who came to see me had a strictly organic difficulty. Another 50 percent had real pain but with a psychosomatic overlay. Some 25 percent of the people I saw over the years had no physical difficulty at all but were suffering from psychosomatic problems. Sometimes simply talking to such a patient is enough to take care of the problem, but oftentimes this is not enough. There is need for more specialized counseling, whether from a psychiatrist, psychologist, social worker, or whatever. The physician needs to work in conjunction with such professionals to treat the patient adequately. I am convinced the medical profession has to recognize that the days of the physician working alone are gone.

In order to achieve this rethinking and to deal with other problem medical areas, physicians have to abandon their attitude of superiority. Unless we see ourselves as ordinary human beings, unless we are willing to listen, to take advice, to change our ways, to work together with others, there is little hope for progress in the much-needed team approach to medicine.

One way for the medical profession to develop a more realistic view of its relationship to its patients as fellow human beings is to insist that the physicians of the future receive a better grounding in liberal arts education. Future doctors need a heavy load of science courses, but they also need solid grounding in disciplines that will help them deal with their patients. An overemphasis on science results in a physician viewing a patient as a pancreas or a liver rather than as a real flesh-and-blood person with feelings. I believe that, in both undergraduate and medical education, future doctors need courses in sociology and history and philosophy, to name but several. Any physician who is to have dealings with black patients should study Afro-American history and culture to provide him—or her—with an understanding of black patients. Understanding the background of black people will allow the doctor to treat them as human beings and not as statistics.

Another way for physicians to become more effective in human relations is to remember that they are often dealing with issues of morality as well as medicine. I consider myself a religious man; I am a deacon in my Baptist church. I believe only a supreme being could have made the world and human beings. I see no conflict between my science and my religious beliefs; the two constantly strengthen one another in my mind. When I look at abortion, euthanasia, and other contemporary medical issues, I make my decisions on both a moral and a scientific basis. I may not always make the right decision, but I always try to keep my patients' humanity in primary view.

Abortion is of course the major socio-medical-moral issue of our day. I see no problem with aborting a fetus within the first twelve weeks of conception, because I see no viability to it up to that point. I oppose abortion after twelve weeks, however, because I believe there is a human life present by that time. I am firmly convinced that, with the wide availability of birth control information, there is no need for any woman to become pregnant unless she wants to. I understand that human nature being what it is, unwanted pregnancies will occur, but not time after time after time. I do not believe in abortion on demand.

I have read about and have been horrified by alleged instances of malformed children being allowed to die. As in the case of machines for the terminally ill, I do not believe heroic measures over and above necessary care must always be administered. If a malformed child or a terminally ill adult cannot survive without the use of machines, I do not believe that machines should be used. But I do not believe in euthanasia, or mercy killing, whether by withholding nourishment from a baby or lethally injecting a drug into an adult. We physicians have an obligation under our Hippocratic Oath to prolong life as long as we can, whenever an individual has a chance to continue living. But we should not administer life-support systems where there is no chance of an individual living without such support.

As physicians we must, of course, be careful not to give up on a patient too soon. The only sure way to know whether a person is dead is through the measurement of brain waves. Unfortunately most hospitals, like ours in Starkville, do not have the equipment to measure these waves, so we must use other determinants. If a person stops breathing and there is no heartbeat on its own after an hour or so of heart stimulation, the person is dead. We can keep the heart pumping artificially, but if the heart cannot do it on its own, then life is no longer present.

I am a firm believer in the need for preventative medical care. I also believe that each person has the ultimate re-

sponsibility for his or her own health. In this vein, though
I smoked myself from my freshman year at Alcorn in 1939
to about 1964, I am totally opposed to smoking or being in
situations where other people do. Tobacco smoke is not an
innocent thing; the smoke going down the lungs is causing
its effect. The best thing anyone can do for his/her health is
to give up the habit immediately.

I also believe that overweight is another major health
problem in this country. However, I worry about the
stigma that we attach to obese people. Such individuals
should be encouraged and not ridiculed; otherwise they
may lose self-esteem as well as the unwanted weight. Each
person should eat a balanced diet and, if health food will
help, then health food is all right. Unfortunately health
food, like megavitamins, has been viewed as a cure-all,
which neither is. In the area of health food, I see no real
danger except that to the pocketbook, but a too-
enthusiastic use of vitamins can cause problems. A and D
vitamins, especially, do not leave the system easily, and
overingestion of them can be dangerous.

Drinking and the use of marijuana and the hard drugs
are other areas for people to consider if they want to preserve their health. I see no health danger to the "social
drinker," the individual who has a drink or two a day.
Anyone who regularly consumes more than that, however, is asking for trouble. Alcoholism is not only a major
health problem in this country; it is also the cause of all
kinds of social problems. As someone who grew up in a
family headed by an alcoholic, I can personally attest to the
harm that alcohol can cause if not handled properly. The
answer to alcohol is education, not prohibition. We must
learn to use liquor properly and teach our children to do
the same. It is a fact of life, and we have to learn how to
deal with it intelligently, not try to ban it in the hope that it
will go away.

A BLACK PHYSICIAN'S STORY

I am opposed to the legalization of marijuana, though I favor a liberalization of the punishment for its use. I do not think anyone should go to jail for smoking the weed; I think a mandatory counseling program makes more sense. My major opposition to marijuana stems directly from science's limited data about its effects. We simply do not know all marijuana's side effects. For example, recent studies indicate that smoking marijuana is even more apt to bring about lung cancer than smoking ordinary cigarettes. I believe much more research is needed before any attempt at legalization can be scientifically justified.

There is absolutely no reason for anyone to become involved with hard drugs. Unfortunately we live in a culture that advocates taking a pill or some sort of a drug to deal with every problem. We as Americans use all kinds of over-the-counter and physician-prescribed drugs as escape mechanisms. As physicians, we too often hurriedly prescribe a drug rather than ask the two or three additional questions that might make such a prescription unnecessary. Our society is accustomed to using prescription drugs to solve physical problems, and too many people view illicit drugs as providing the same benefit. They don't, but their use tragically increases anyway.

The growth of this drug culture is probably the greatest threat to Americans' health that I have seen develop during my professional lifetime. The hectic pace of all of our lives does not encourage me that we, as a society, will take the time to deal with the problem as we should. As long as Americans rush through life, the temptation to use drugs to tranquilize or to energize will continue to be a problem.

I can see the effects of the hectic pace of modern life on my patients, most of whom, thankfully, do not abuse drugs. Too many people do not do the basic things that are vital for a long, healthy life. They do not eat regular meals, they do not sleep regularly, they eat too much, they do not

100

get enough exercise, and they worry too much. Their lives are hectic rather than calm. I am a classic example of the old saying: "Do as I say, not as I do." Or perhaps, "Physician, heal thyself" is more appropriate. My own life has been and continues to be hectic. I have received a great deal of fulfillment out of my profession, and I do not want to slow down or retire when I reach sixty-five. Instead, my dream is to find a young doctor to join me as an associate and then continue practicing at a less hectic pace. I would like to stop seeing thirty to forty patients a day and see only about twelve instead. I would like to be able to deal with patients in a more relaxed atmosphere, so that I might give each one all the time that he or she needs. I have a prospect who seems interested in joining me, but if he does not come, I will probably continue to conduct my practice as I have for the last thirty-odd years. If this is the way it is to be, I will not complain. I like what I do, and I want to keep doing it as long as I have the physical and mental capacity to do so.

As I look back on my professional career so far, I am happy that it has been all I had dreamed it would be when I was a young child in Hattiesburg dispensing bottles of colored water to imaginary patients. I believe I have been able to help improve conditions for black people and bring hope to one corner of Mississippi. Were I to go back and begin my medical career again, I can think of nothing I would do differently except spend more time with my family.

7
STATE AND NATIONAL POLITICS

During the thirty-four years that I have practiced medicine in Starkville, I have also been involved in politics at the local, state, and national level. I have participated in the founding of the local chapter of the National Association for the Advancement of Colored People and have been involved in various local efforts to end discrimination. I have served on numerous local and state committees, and on two occasions was invited to meetings at the White House. My political, civic, and integration activities were all the result of my desire to make things better, to bring hope to black people in my community.

From my earliest days in Starkville, I was not happy with race relations there. It seemed to me the community was even more polarized than I remembered Hattiesburg being. Starkville in the 1950s and early 1960s was thoroughly segregated. Separate-but-equal did not exist. Usually blacks were excluded. When we were allowed to use the same facilities as whites, we were placed in insulting situations which were meant to emphasize our subordination. The schools, of course, were segregated. The complex that today is the integrated Henderson Junior High School was then the black-only Oktibbeha County Training School. Whites had their own schools, and, needless to say, the white facilities were far superior to the black ones.

Blacks did not have the opportunity to hold meaningful jobs. There were a few black businessmen in town, but most blacks had to take whatever menial position was available, either in Starkville or at the neighboring college. All over town one could see blacks sweeping and mopping, but rarely was a black seen in a business suit. There were no black bank tellers, no black government clerks, and certainly no black college professors.

Everywhere blacks went, they encountered segregation. If they wanted to eat at a restaurant, the white ones were closed to them except perhaps for the back door. The few black restaurants were nothing more than sandwich shops. The only movie theater in town was the Rex (today, a lawyer's office). If blacks wanted to see a movie, they had to sit in the balcony, the so-called buzzard's roost. At times, they would vent their frustrations by throwing popcorn down on the white patrons below. The ushers would then come charging up the stairs, and there would be a big stew and wrangle.

When blacks went shopping, they saw no black salespersons and they encountered all kinds of rudeness. At clothing stores we were discouraged from trying anything on. We were supposed to hold the clothes against our bodies to try to determine correct fit. Sometimes, if a black insisted and if there were no white customers around, a store clerk might allow him or her to go to the back of the store and actually try something on.

As I have indicated earlier, segregation was also part of Starkville's medical scene. I was the only black doctor in town, and there were no black dentists. Most dental offices had segregated waiting rooms, and one dentist was known to do extractions in his black waiting room rather than allow blacks to enter his treatment area. His "separate-but-equal" black treatment facilities seemed to consist of a washbasin for use in the black waiting room.

Voting in Starkville was open only to a few blacks. In the early 1950s businessmen like Uncle Rob Wier, George Evans, Ernest Jones, B. L. Robinson, Clarence Taylor, and Ferdinand Barry were allowed to vote, but they normally voted early in the morning so that as few whites as possible saw them at the polls.

As soon as I arrived I went to the county courthouse to begin the registration process. I received some startled looks, but I was allowed to pay my poll tax. I then had to wait a year, go back, pay the poll tax again, show my poll tax receipt from the previous year, and finally be registered. No one asked me to interpret the Constitution or do anything else; I never heard of that kind of thing going on in Starkville. The poll tax—and a clear understanding that blacks were not supposed to vote—kept most blacks from even trying to register. I encouraged everyone I could to register, but most people were afraid to do so. The police had a reputation for arresting blacks with little cause and then treating them roughly, so most blacks did not want to do anything that might antagonize the authorities.

The neighboring Mississippi A and M College (now Mississippi State University) did not have a positive effect on the town's race relations. Normally one would think that a college would provide a liberalizing effect, that it would be in the forefront of racial justice and equality, but such was not the case there. Except for a few isolated individuals, the college provided no leadership in this area. It observed the segregation customs like everyone else.

Generally, the only black presence on campus was in some sort of menial role. A few blacks attended the college's athletic events, but they had to stand behind the goalposts during the football games or around the edges of the court during basketball games. After a big football victory, blacks had to take care not to be caught on the city's streets. College students celebrated victories by go-

104

ing on rampages which frequently included pranks like throwing eggs at blacks.

When I arrived in Starkville in 1951, I noted the anti-black effects of the community, but I was wrapped up in my practice and beginning my family and had little time to concern myself with anything else. My days consisted of taking care of patients, not fighting discrimination. In the back of my mind, however, I pondered what I saw and wished I could do something to change it. I remembered my childhood determination to try to fight segregation head-on.

It was sometime in the late 1950s that my conscience received its major jolt. Medgar Evers, the state field secretary of the National Association for the Advancement of Colored People, came to town to see me and several other black leaders. He arrived without fanfare because this was his style. He was a quiet, introspective man, the direct opposite of his brother Charles. I sometimes wondered how he became involved in civil rights activities, as calm and peaceful as he was, but it was precisely this quiet persistence that made him so effective.

When Medgar came to Starkville, he visited me in my office and we discussed the racial situation of that day. He said: "Conner, Starkville needs a chapter of the NAACP. You would be a good one to start it up." "Well," I replied, "I've been thinking about that myself. I'll think it over some more." "In the meantime," Medgar replied, "why don't you start by beginning a life membership in the NAACP?" I agreed and gave him fifty dollars. That was about it. He put no pressure on me; he simply made the suggestions and left town as quietly as he had arrived.

After he left I did a lot of thinking. I told myself that I agreed with what he had said. Perhaps, I thought, I'm spending too much time with my patients and not as much time as I should trying to better the community for other blacks. If things are ever to get better, I thought, I have to become more active in groups and organizations that work for human rights. I talked to others Medgar had visited and other blacks in the community about beginning a NAACP chapter, but we had no success until the late 1960s.

During the late 1950s and early 1960s I sometimes went to NAACP state meetings in Jackson with Dr. E. J. Stringer, a Columbus dentist, but no one else from Starkville went. State meetings in those days mainly consisted of discussing ways to start new chapters. Sometimes someone would ask about Oktibbeha County, and I would always say, "We're working on it." Actually, nothing was being done.

It was in the mid-1960s that the first stirrings of protest began to be felt in Starkville. Passage of the federal Voting Rights Act in 1965 pompted Starkville blacks to begin thinking of voting in large numbers for the first time. I continued my practice of encouraging blacks to register, and could now bolster my encouragement by pointing to the new legislation. But many still felt too intimidated to try to register, so around 1967 or 1968 we requested that federal registrars be sent into the city. They set up a temporary office in the Post Office Building. Some blacks were willing to go there to register whereas they were afraid to go to the courthouse. Old fears and practices die hard. The result of our efforts was a large increase in the number of black voters.

Meanwhile, in Mississippi as a whole the state was afire with civil rights activities. In 1962 James Meredith integrated the University of Mississippi and during those years three civil rights workers were murdered and Freedom Summer took place. Mississippi became the watchword for white southern resistance to integration.

In 1964 this resistance was dramatized on television

when the Freedom Democratic Party, a coalition of civil rights organizations, appeared before the national Democratic Convention demanding recgnition and seating in place of the regular white-only state Democratic Party delegation. When Fannie Lou Hamer made her famous speech, the nation listened in rapt attention. Lyndon Johnson controlled this meeting and helped devise a compromise that he hoped would settle the matter to everyone's satisfaction. He proposed seating the Regulars and giving the Freedom Democrats two seats—one each for Aaron Henry and Ed King. At the same time, the party drafted a resolution making it clear that the 1968 convention would accredit only nondiscriminatory delegations. The FDP refused the solution, but in 1968, when the Regulars still refused to integrate, the Freedom Democrats were seated.

I was not involved in politics in those days, and consequently all my information on the 1964 convention and the later conflict between the FDP and the Loyalists is secondhand. What I heard and read, however, was that there never was much unity of purpose among the Freedom Democrats except for their determination to receive national convention recognition. There was, however, general agreement on tactics. The FDP wanted to be all-black and take noncompromising stands on issues. Other blacks and whites disagreed. They believed in integration and black participation in politics as the FDP did, but thought it should be achieved by blacks and whites working together. People like Aaron Henry argued that if there was ever going to be any real progress in the state it would be achieved only through racial cooperation, not through polarization. So he and others began organizing an integrated black-white Democratic Party, whose members later came to be called the Loyalist Democrats. There were a lot of political battles between the FDP and the Loyalists, always over tactics. After a time the Loyalists' more conservative integration approach won out over the Freedom Democrats' more radical black-only approach. After the 1968 national convention, the black-white Loyalists became the major state political force opposing the white-only Regulars.

I was never a member of the Freedom Democratic Party. I was not participating in politics in those days, and the FDP never made any attempt to draw me in. When the Loyalists began organizing the state in earnest after the 1968 convention, however, Aaron Henry, who knew me from my attendance at state NAACP and North Mississippi Medical, Dental, and Pharmaceutical Association meetings, asked me to join the Loyalists. Since the newly organized party was so new, there were few established people. Consequently, when I joined I immediately became a member of the Loyalist Executive Committee, a post I held in the merged party until 1984 when the requirement to have a balance of whites and blacks, men and women prevented my re-election.

There were about fourteen members on that original committee, both whites and blacks. We were mostly black, but whites like Hodding Carter III, Pat Derian, and Wes Watkins ignored the label "nigger lover" and became part of the party too. Most white Democrats remained Regulars, however, and from 1968 until the merger in 1976 there were two Democratic factions in the state: the white liberal and mostly black Loyalists and the white male, over forty, "set in their ways" Regulars

The Executive Committee of the Loyalist Democratic Party primarily set policy for the state and county organizations. The Executive Committee ran the party in cooperation with state chairman Aaron Henry. The committee also sent to the local levels policy and materials coming down from the national party. We conducted the caucuses that elected delegates to the national convention. We ran primary elections to try to ensure the selection of representative candidates. We tried to do whatever was necessary to make sure that our party prospered. We had ultimate authority over Democratic politics in the state (though the existence of the competing Regulars meant this control was not exclusive.)

In addition to fighting the Regulars, or perhaps because of the existence of the split, we always had money problems. This was my special concern because, in addition to being a member of the Executive Committee, I was also party treasurer. It was an almost impossible job. Each of the county organizations was asssessed a certain amount of money for support of the state party, but few were totally successful in raising their assigned sums. We were always in the red. We could never gather enough funds to do all the things we wanted to do, and many of us had to dig into our own pockets to keep the party going. I know Aaron Henry incurred a substantial debt just maintaining the party headquarters at Clarksdale. But somehow, we survived. From 1968 until the merger in 1976 I was involved in round after round of meetings to try to generate money to keep the party afloat.

In 1971 I was on the Loyalist committee which tried unsuccessfully to get the Regulars to merge. They refused to respond to this and other similar overtures. It was not until 1976 that pressure from the national party produced union. Both sides came to see that, considering our financial problems and the growth of a serious Republican opposition, it was foolish to keep two Democratic factions existing on the ashes of past problems. Today there are no Regulars and no Loyalists; there is one Democratic state party in Mississippi.

The formula for successful merger came from the national party, on the advice of Aaron Henry. The plan was the dual chairperson system. Aaron and Tom Ridell, a

Loyalist and a Regular, became co-chairmen of the unified party. Every party committee likewise had co-chairs—black and white, women and men. For example, I became co-chairman of the Affirmative Action Committee.

This system remained in effect until 1980, when Governor William Winter mandated that we go to a one-chairperson organization. On the surface, his action seemed to make sense. You can't have two chairpersons; you either have a chairperson or you don't have a chairperson. Actually, the two-chair method was about the only way to merge the two parties, which had been poles apart for so long. If we had decided to go with only one chairperson, either some white or some black, some Loyalist or some Regular would have been offended. The co-chair idea was excellent for bringing the two groups together with the least difficulty. True, there were in effect two parties in existence at the same time, but the concept worked well and it was a real education for everyone involved.

My own experience might make my point clearer. I was co-chairman of the Affirmative Action Committee with a George Wallace supporter from Kosciusko, a real resin-chewing red-neck named Terry Haimes. When I first learned of this situation, I asked myself: "How can I ever co-chair a committee with a guy who voted for Wallace?" But I decided to try. It's amazing how a person can learn to work with others if actually placed in the situation. My co-chairing experience with Terry Haimes gave me a chance to get to know him and to find out that he is a decent human being. I could not have learned this otherwise. I would have continued thinking of him only as a Wallace supporter and seeing him as an adversary.

I believe that it was a mistake to end the two-chair system. One of the results of having only one chairperson in Mississippi is that invariably the chairperson is white.

There are now fewer blacks in leadership positions than there were before. I remained on the Executive Committee and kept my job as the chairman of the Second Congressional District, a post I had held since 1968. In 1980 I also became chairman of the Election Committee. Unfortunately, many other blacks lost their leadership roles.

I held two chairmanships until 1984. As head of the Election Committee, my job was to coordinate the certification of Democratic candidates, primary results, and their announcement. We also tried to stimulate voter education and registration to increase the size of the state party. Additionally, we tried to convince the state legislature to pass bills that are in the best interests of our party. In this area we had only limited success. We were able to persuade the legislature to allow votes for presidential candidates and not for electors pledged to them. We were also able to get the legislature to shorten the qualifying time for congressional candidates. On the other hand, our proposals for Saturday elections and state income tax deductions for political contributions failed.

My job as chairman of the Second Congressional District, which I held until Starkville became part of the Third District in 1984, was not as powerful as it might seem. Democratic and Republican politics mean very little in Mississippi on the local level. Persons running for local office rarely run as Democrats or Republicans. Consequently, I played practically no role in local elections in my position as district party chairman. During the days when there was a split I tried to encourage blacks in areas of black majorities to run as Democrats and not as Independents. There was a good bit of talk in the late sixties and early seventies about ignoring both parties and starting an independent black party instead. I opposed this idea then and worked to undercut it wherever it arose in my district.

The major task of the district chairperson is to preside

111

over the selection of delegates to the national convention every four years. Normally, Democrats first meet at the county level and select delegates to the district caucus. At the district level, delegates are elected to the national convention. My major job as district chairman has been to preside over these district gatherings and ensure a fair election of delegates. These individuals, along with those selected at the state convention, represent Mississippi Democrats at the national nominating convention.

As district chairman I have had an obvious advantage when it has come to selecting national convention delegates. During the three presidential elections held during my chairmanship, I was elected a district delegate twice—in 1972 and 1980. In 1976 I supported former Oklahoma Senator Fred Harris, and since he had almost no support in the district, I lost out. That year I was picked as a delegate during the state convention. My participation in Democratic politics as a Loyalist and as a member of the merged party resulted in my attendance at national nominating conventions in 1972, 1976, and 1980. I was also a delegate to the two recent national conferences—the one in 1978 and the one in 1982. I was not a delegate to the 1984 national convention because the requirement to have a proportionate number of men and women, blacks and whites prevented my election. I did, however, attend the convention as a spectator.

I was able to go to three national conventions because I could afford the cost. A delegate receives no financial support from the state party; he or she must foot the considerable cost from his or her own pocket. Based on my three experiences, I would estimate that in the 1980s the cost for a Mississippi delegate to attend the 1984 national convention was about $1,500, a substantial sum of money. Needless to say, this cost automatically limits the people who can become delegates. When the Loyalists were going to the national conventions, we elected delegates irrespective of financial ability and then found ways to cover their expenses. Sometimes we received help from the national party. Electing delegates without considering their financial status made our delegations representative. Since the merger, however, we have not been able to continue finding financial support for delegates without sufficient means of their own. Consequently, there are some people who will not even run for delegate because they recognize they cannot afford to go to the convention, even if elected. I worry that our delegation is not as representative as it should be, and I wish we could find some way to deal with this situation.

Delegates must also be prepared to devote time and money to the inevitable preconvention maneuvering. Each time, before the Mississippi delegation's departure for the convension city, we have met together in Jackson to plan our strategy and determine our delegation's positions on vital issues. In the weeks before leaving we will have received congratulatory letters from aspiring candidates and packets of information indicating why we should support this or that person's candidacy. Our minds are usually made up by this time, but the information has been helpful, nonetheless, in comparing candidates and studying the issues.

Once a delegation arrives at the convention city, the excitement begins. Being a delegate to a national nominating convention is a stirring experience. We are on the go from the minute we arise in the early morning to the late hour we finally go to bed. We caucus often as a delegation—and with delegates from other states when the circumstances demand it. Normally our hotel is some distance from the convention center, so we are bused back and forth, morning and evening. We spend most of our time on the convention floor, sitting in the seats assigned to our state delegation, but the floor is in such a state of pandemonium that we can hardly hear anything. There is a constant noise—delegates and media people pacing the floor back and forth, up and down. It is even difficult to hear the speaker at the podium.

Most of the time, in fact, the action is on the floor and not at the podium. Speakers drone on, one after another, and if anyone really wants to hear what someone is saying, he or she can simply read the text that is usually made available or stand in front of one of the television sets located everywhere. Most of the time delegates are caucusing and establishing coalitions. Or they are busy meeting and talking to old friends. The news media seem to be everywhere. Let any prominent figure appear and that person will quickly be trailed by a newsman or newswoman with TV cameras in tow. The average delegate is rarely the target of media people, but it is fun, nonetheless, to watch famous political and news figures in action.

The convention itself is programmed. Nobody gains access to the podium without permission. In most instances, opposing views are stifled; dissidents are kept from the microphones. National party leaders want a smooth-flowing convention. The last thing they want to do is give the public any impression of Democratic feuding. What disagreement there is, and sometimes there is a great deal of it, takes place in the caucuses and conferences away from the television eye. The convention is structured to nominate a candidate in the least controversial way, so that he can begin his campaign with no public misconceptions about his party's support for him.

And so, as average delegates we usually don't have to worry about anything but casting our votes for the candidate of our choice and mingling with other average delegates to gain ideas to take home and use in our own state. Each delegation is situated near three or four other state delegations, so there is a great deal of moving back and forth and much exchanging of thoughts. I remember in 1972 that our Mississippi delegation was located behind the Florida group. We were the Loyalists, and they were staunch Wallace supporters. Needless to say, we had some spirited discussions, friendly but determined. Neither of us convinced the other, but we had a chance to learn their ideas, and they had a chance to learn ours.

Unfortunately the average delegate does not usually have the opportunity to meet the candidates. Most of the time the candidates are in their hotel rooms or trailer command posts outside the convention building. Normally they don't come to the convention floor or podium unless they have something crucial to say about their candidacy. When they do come, the news media so surround them that they have little chance to mingle with the delegates at large. Most candidates will greet each member of their home state delegations, but that's about it. Jimmy Carter was unique in shaking hands with every delegate during one convention.

My choices during the three conventions I attended indicate my political philosophy, which I consider to be liberal, or slightly left of center. In 1972 I supported George McGovern. In 1976 my heart was with Teddy Kennedy, but I was pledged to vote for Carter on the first ballot. I found myself in the same situation in 1980. It was not that I did not like Carter because I did—and do. I was happy to see a southerner win the nomination and then the presidency. But I felt that Kennedy stood for more of the things that I considered important. So I believed that he deserved my support in 1976 and 1980, even though I could not deliver because of my commitment to Carter.

I did not attend the 1984 Democratic convention as a delegate, going only as a spectator, but I participated in both the primary and the general election campaigns. I supported Walter Mondale throughout. I concentrated my efforts on the local level as a member of the Oktibbeha County Executive Committee in charge of telephoning potential voters and organizing rides to the polls on Election Day. Mondale lost the county, some seven thousand to five thousand, but this margin was a lot closer than most people had predicted.

I really don't believe that any Democrat could have beaten Ronald Reagan in 1984. Reagan is very likable; he's an actor; and he knows how to use the media. His highly organized campaign made sophisticated use of all the latest media techniques. The Democratic campaign, by comparison, always seemed to be a little disorganized, and after the early Labor endorsement of Mondale it was perceived as too closely tied to "special interests." The nomination of Geraldine Ferraro did not help either, especially in the South. She ran a good campaign, but too many southerners, both men and women, believe that a woman should look pretty, but she should never have a thought in her mind and should certainly never run for the vice presidency.

Then there was Jesse Jackson. At first I had serious misgivings about his running. I believed he had no chance to gain the nomination, and his candidacy would cause such a division in the party that it would have difficulty coming together behind the party's nominee. To a degree, I was right. A lot of blacks, particularly younger ones, had never registered or voted before and came out in droves to support Jackson. They were determined to get him the nomination, but when he lost they could not support Walter Mondale with the same vigor.

In the long run, however, Jesse Jackson's candidacy was a positive factor. His running helped instill a sense of pride in many younger blacks, convincing them that some day there would be a black president. I caught a lot of flak from some blacks for not supporting Jackson. But I remained convinced that Walter Mondale had the best chance of any of the candidates the Democrats could nominate. I gave money to the Jackson campaign and I was proud of all he did, but I supported Mondale.

In the final analysis, however, it was neither Mondale, nor Organized Labor, nor Ferraro, nor Jackson that made the difference. Ronald Reagan was simply unbeatable. He would have defeated anyone the Democrats threw at him. The campaign was over even before it began. Reagan had it won from the day he gained the Republican nomination.

Reagan's landslide victory will have a significance far into the future, and I'm afraid that significance will be negative. I believe Ronald Reagan's second term will witness more and more deprivation of the poor. Reagan seems determined to cut back or eliminate all federal social programs, and the American people don't seem to understand that such cuts will have a devastating effect not only on the poor but on the community as a whole. Both blacks and whites, for example, will suffer from Reagan's determination to cut back on aid to education.

Participating in politics as I have, I have noted how Democratic Party attitudes have changed over the years. In 1972 the thrust of the party was "Let's help the poor! Let's throw the door open! You can't give enough to people who are disadvantaged." In recent years, I believe the party has become more responsible. We have become more careful about espousing programs. We now study them more carefully to make sure that they deliver what they promise, that they really do help the poor lift themselves up by their bootstraps. Democrats have not become less caring; we have become more careful.

But we have not adopted Republican attitudes on the issue of aiding the downtrodden. I remain convinced that there is a real difference between Democrats and Repub-

117

licans on most domestic issues. Democrats want to give opportunity to the disadvantaged by making sure that the federal dollar does what it was intended to do. Republicans remain more interested in pleasing Wall Street than in taking care of those in need. Ronald Reagan's policy calls for eliminating federal programs which help the poor and doing everything to help those with the most money, hoping that benefits will eventually trickle-down to the poor and needy. Democrats do not believe in trickle-down; we believe in direct aid for those who need it most. Our challenge after the 1984 election is to convince the American people that we are a party whose programs will benefit the entire nation and not just a few supposed special interests. In some ways Gary Hart tried to say this in 1984, but he did it in such an erratic, sporadic way that the message never reached the listeners.

I believe that the best thing Democrats can do is concentrate not on lopping off all federal social programs as Ronald Reagan wants to do but in reforming these programs so that they provide an incentive to help people become economically independent. Rather than maintaining programs that perpetuate dead-end welfare, Democrats need to provide programs that move people from dependence to independence. It can be done, and when it is done, I am convinced the Democrats will be the ones who do it.

Democrats also have a more enlightened view on racial issues than Republicans do. I know from experience that there were and still are racists in my own state party, but the thrust of the national party is definitely positive. Republican state and national policy, on the other hand, seems to be antiblack despite the presence of some fair-minded party members. I even voted for a Republican in a state election because I respect him so much. I voted for

Gil Carmichael when he ran for governor and later for lieutenant governor. I believe he is a good man, a decent man, without any obvious signs of racial prejudice. I thought that if he gained public office he could help move the state Republican Party in a more racially liberal direction. Unfortunately Carmichael lost each time he ran, and the Republican Party is even more conservative than it was. It continues to reflect national GOP antiblack politics accurately.

The Democratic Party, on the other hand, has really tried to open up since 1964, going out of its way to be meaningful to blacks, women, and the poor. Democrats have tried to ensure that all elements of American society are represented in party councils, even spelling out in the party constitution that state parties have to be fair to all. For a time we Democrats even tried proportionate representation, but this has now gone by the wayside. I wish we could go back to it. I wish we had a way to make sure that blacks, Hispanics, and other minorities are represented in the party hierarchy in proportion to their numbers in the general population. Some argue that this is a quota system and wrong; I say that it is democracy at work and only right.

My participation at conventions and at the two conferences has been a positive experience. The conferences were basically designed as morale boosters, but I found them very valuable anyway. There was no presidential politicking, so we were able to concentrate on establishing party positions on the major problems of the time. Each time I have left a convention or a conference I have been fired up to come back to Mississippi and make the state party more meaningful, to pattern the state party's procedures and policies on those of other successful states. In this way I believe participation in conventions and conferences is important to anyone involved in state politics. It provides the information and the boost to make that involvement more significant.

After the 1972 national nominating convention I came back to an impossible job. Patricia Derian and I were made the state co-chairpersons of the McGovern for President campaign in Mississippi. Those were still the days of the Loyalist-Regular split, and the regulars wanted nothing to do with McGovern. He was not very popular in Mississippi as a whole, and this meant that Pat and I had our work cut out for us. The entire Loyalist organization helped, of course, but Pat and I had the major roles. She lived in the Jackson area, so she did most of the work; I went down every week or so, and she called me regularly so we could make major decisions together.

Looking back on that campaign now, I believe McGovern wrote Mississippi off from the beginning. He never even visited the state, though his running mate, Sargent Shriver, did. Most of our effort consisted of issuing press statements, passing along instructions from the national headquarters, deciding how to spend our limited funds most efficiently, and determining which speaker to send to which public appearance. There was a lot of hard work and very little glamour in the job.

I have also been active in other presidential and statewide campaigns. I have made speeches in the Golden Triangle region of Starkville, Columbus, and West Point; I have helped raise money; I have helped organize telephone banks to reach potential voters; I have even been a poll watcher. I have done all the things that are essential if the political party system is to be successful.

I have also had the opportunity to visit the White House. In 1970 Richard Nixon appointed me a member of the Mississippi State Advisory Committee to the Cabinet Committee on Education, the first of seven Deep South

Dr. Douglas Conner with President Richard Nixon at a White House Conference 24 June 1970

committees to try to ensure peaceful integration of the public schools in the South. The Mississippi committee was in existence from 1970 until 1973 and had sixteen members, ten whites and six blacks—businessmen, physicians, and ministers. There was a white chairman, a black vice-chairman, and a white secretary.

The Mississippi committee, along with those from the other southern states, went to the White House for a meeting on June 24, 1970. As it turned out, the whole affair

121

proved long on ceremony and short on substance. President Nixon came in and made a bland statement. Each of us then met the president, shook hands with him, and had our picture taken with him. Once this was over, he left and his staff took over. Again, little of substance was discussed. I came away from the meeting viewing Nixon as more human and friendly than I had pictured him to be, but with no new insights on our committee's duties toward school integration.

I soon learned that the reason for the emptiness of the White House gathering was that the Nixon administration only wanted us to be a showcase. My fellow committee members were honorable men, but our meetings for the next three years were as unproductive as the White House gathering. We listened to reports on the progress of integration from state and a few federal officials, but we had very little input during the presentations. We were there to listen, not to offer ideas. It was a sham, a showcase, and nothing more. Integration took place in Mississippi, but in many areas whites moved to segregated academies and left the public schools to black students. So we failed at our main aim of making the state a model of integration and preventing the proliferation of academies at the expense of the public school systems. Still, any biracial committee in Mississippi produces some good simply by its being biracial. By that standard, our committee produced some good too.

My second visit to the White House came during the administration of Jimmy Carter. A black staff member named Louis Martin (who had also formerly served with Kennedy and Johnson) set up an October 25, 1978, meeting of black leaders from all over the South to meet Carter and hear firsthand what his administration had done for blacks. Again, the affair was largely ceremonial. President Carter came in, said a few words, and again there was an

Dr. Douglas Conner with President Jimmy Carter at a White House Conference 25 October, 1978

individual picture-taking session. Carter then left and his staff recited the names of all the blacks he had appointed to positions of authority in his administration, in the judicial system, and so forth. Like Nixon, Carter was very pleasant, and although I think a great deal more of him and his record than I do of Nixon's, I must say that this meeting, like the one with Nixon, was not very substantial.

Though neither of my meetings in the White House was of real significance, both occasions were memorable expe-

123

riences. I felt a sense of awe looking around, recalling the history of the place, and realizing that I was there. The thought of my beginnings and where I was then standing was overwhelming. Just a few years previously, a black man like me would never have had the opportunity to enter the White House, let alone be among other blacks and whites as a guest of honor. Clearly, I thought, the American political system had made some gigantic strides—despite the many needs that still existed.

On the state level in Mississippi, progress has been much slower. Our politicians have not embraced the changes as quickly as have the nation's presidents. Our governors from the 1950s to the present were a mixed bag. They ranged from enlightened individuals like the man who served as governor of the state from 1980 to 1984, Willian Winter, to racial demagogues like Ross Barnett and John Bell Williams. Our senators and congressmen, with the exception of ex-congressman Frank Smith, have not been in the forefront of the battle for freedom. In the 1960s Senators James Eastland and John Stennis were leaders in opposition to civil rights legislation. Eastland never changed as far as I could see. Stennis, on the other hand, surprised me in 1982 by voting for the extension of the Voting Rights Act. Political considerations caused this change, indicating the growing importance of the black vote in Mississippi.

In 1982 I worked for the reelection of John Stennis to the United States Senate. Some people were taken aback when I approached them to vote and work for Stennis. "Doug Conner," they asked, "how can *you* back Stennis?" I always responded the same way: "After all, the old man did vote for the extension of the Voting Rights Act. I much prefer to have a conservative Democrat in the Congress who, unlike a conservative Republican, will not rubber-stamp everything Ronald Reagan does." All things being equal, I will always support Democrats because I believe our party has more to offer the nation than the Republicans do. As long as the party and its officials are fair to me and to black people generally, I plan to remain a Democrat and support its candidates.

I must say, though, that in recent years several things happened that I found upsetting. I was most disturbed when the then-Governor Winter, whom I consider the most progressive Mississippi governor in my lifetime, insisted on ending the two-chair system and handpicking a white chairman. The result has been fewer party leadership positions for blacks.

The unsuccessful 1982 race of black party leader Robert Clark in the new Delta congressional district was also upsetting. Democratic white leaders came out for Clark, but they did not seem to use their full political clout to deliver the votes to him. Local Democratic leaders publicly supported Clark for the House and Stennis for the Senate, but in private I suspect their support for Clark was weak. I believe they spread the word that it was all right to vote for the Republican candidate in the House race, as long as people voted for Stennis in the Senate race.

I realize that Clark also suffered black defections. Black mayors in one county in his district urged blacks to stay at home to punish him for not coming out more strongly in support of Eddie Carthan, a black mayor on trial for the alleged murder of a political opponent. There were two sides to Clark's 1982 defeat, but I believe that the lack of true white support rather than some black defections was the major reason for his defeat.

In the aftermath of 1982, I and many other blacks were openly worried whether the state Democratic party could ever be truly meaningful to poor whites and blacks. I heard many disappointed blacks begin talking about going the Independent route and supporting either Republicans or Democrats on the state level, depending on which candidates looked best to them. I felt the same way, frustrated at what I saw was the state party's willingness to condone the defeat of a good man with wide experience simply because he was black.

I watched Clark's 1984 campaign very closely, and though he lost I noted that the Democratic party on the state level did all it could to help get him elected. All the state's leading Democrats, with the exception of Stennis, endorsed Clark and tried to aid him in any way they could. I and most other blacks were encouraged that black protests over the state party's 1982 attitude had helped bring about this change. Our faith in the future of the state party was restored. We were disappointed Clark lost, but we believe this happened because of the Reagan landslide, not the indifference of state Democrats.

8
LOCAL POLITICS

During the years I have been involved in the state Democratic Party, I have also participated in local politics. The period has seen a quiet revolution take place in Starkville. The passage of the federal Voting Rights Act of 1965 and our own local registration efforts in the late 1960s resulted in an emerging Starkville and Oktibbeha County black electorate. Many more than a mere handful of black leaders were now able to vote, but we had no idea of the exact number of blacks on the registration lists. If this body of new black registrants was to be an effective force, it had to be identified and organized.

In the late 1960s and early 1970s I helped stimulate an effort to organize the newly enfranchised black voters. Throughout all of our efforts, however, we kept running into a major problem: the Oktibbeha County circuit clerk refused to allow us to look at the voter registration books. These lists are, of course, public and supposed to be open to everyone, but he refused our repeated requests to see them. Consequently, in 1971 Bennie Butler and I sued him in U.S. District Court. We received a court order in May 1971 giving us—and, for that matter, any other citizen— the right to look at the registration books. The circuit clerk remained reluctant, but he had no choice. He opened the books to us.

We spent a good bit of time studying the rolls, identifying voters, making lists, and in general determining the black-white makeup of the registered voters in Oktibbeha County. We knew that, according to the 1970 census, the county's population was 28,752 and that of this number 35 percent were black. We also knew that the total number of persons of voting age (twenty-one and over) was 15,135. Of this number, only 30 percent were black. By studying the voting rolls with the help of residents from each voting district, we found that, of the 11,033 registered voters, only 3,075 or 28 percent were black.

These were, of course, discouraging figures, indicating that blacks were a distinct voting minority in the county. Any black candidate would have to face overwhelming odds to gain a countywide office. A breakdown of the county according to individual beats was equally discouraging. Whites outnumbered black voters by a wide margin in all five beats of the county. We were a population and voting minority in the county as a whole and in every beat within it.

Had we thought about it at the time, we would have found we had a right to be encouraged. Before the passage of the Voting Rights Act and our local registration drive, there had been only a handful of registered black voters. Most blacks had not even considered the possibility of voting. Yet by 1971 there were 3,075 registered black voters. The voting rolls had changed from being nearly all white to being 28 percent black. Even more encouraging should have been the realization that we had registered 70 percent of the blacks in the county twenty-one years of age or over. By contrast, whites had registered 74 percent of their same age group. Considering all the obstacles we had had to overcome, we should have realized that we had accomplished much in a short time.

128

The only numbers we considered were the totals of black versus white voters. We could not rationalize away the fact that there were 7,958 white voters to only 3,075 black voters. The only way any black candidate could ever expect to gain an election victory was to get out all the black voters and receive their votes while entering a significant number of white votes too. It was a near impossibility, but running for office was the next step we blacks had to take if we were ever to play a significant role in community life. Besides, no black could ever gain political office if no black ever ran.

I decided to take my chances and ran for elective office three times: first in 1971 for the state Senate, then for the Starkville Board of Aldermen in 1973, and finally for the state legislature in 1975. In all three instances I lost, but the effort was not a wasted one. I knew from the start that I had little hope of winning. I was among the first black candidates to seek public office in Oktibbeha County. I certainly wanted to win each time I ran, but I knew my main contribution in running would be to raise black consciousness. I wanted to show that blacks could and should run for political office. Although I lost all three races, I do believe I accomplished my task and paved the way for the winning black candidates who have followed me.

My three decisions to run for office were not made without a good deal of thought. I knew that, should I somehow win, I would have to rethink my professional and private life. I would be busier than ever and would have to make the necessary allowances. I knew, for example, that should I win election to the legislature I would have to make arrangements for another physician to cover for me during the weekdays of the legislature's three-month session. I knew, too, that I would have to do a great deal of traveling back and forth to Jackson and that I would be in constant demand by my constituents. However, I decided to run anyway. I believed I had a duty to do so.

I conducted all my campaigns about the same way. I did not have a real political organization; I pretty much ran everything myself, though I received help from relatives and from friends in the local NAACP chapter. I realize now that I made a mistake in not organizing better, but that was the way I did it. Each time, I first helped organize a voter registration drive. With the cooperation of the NAACP and local churches, I helped instruct blacks how to register and how to vote. In this way I tried to ensure a maximum number of black voters to support my candidacy at election time.

I did not conduct any elaborate fund-raising activities other than dinners and fish fries at local churches. Consequently, I always ended up running with limited funds; my campaigns were conducted on a shoestring. I used no television ads, no computer printouts, and no door-to-door campaigning. My medical practice simply did not allow me enough time to meet the voters at their doorsteps. Instead , I used a few radio spots at the end of each of the campaigns, announcements in the local newspapers, speeches at local churches, and, most importantly, position papers on pertinent issues. I concentrated on presenting my candidacy to the voters on a rational basic, rather than then appealing to their emotions.

Race was, of course, a major issue in each of my campaigns, and I tried to meet it head-on. I appealed for white as well as for black votes. I had to have both. Some of my handouts had a sketch of a white hand shaking a black hand. Every chance I had, I stressed the fact that a person's race made no difference to me. I promised not to show any racial partiality. I said I would try to provide opportunities for both blacks and whites. I particularly tried to calm any white concern over an alleged black takeover. I emphasized that my election was not part of a black effort to exclude whites. I portrayed myself as I truly believed I was: one man trying to bridge the gap between black and white.

While meeting the racial issue head-on, I nevertheless tried not to overemphasize it. When I first announced my decision to run for the state Senate in 1971, I included the following paragraph near the end of my published opening statement:

> I seek the office of State Senator not as a black or as a white Mississippian—but as a Mississippian (Period). I am vitally interested in all races and all people working together to build a state that is second to none—to build a Mississippi with the highest per capita income in the nation—to build a Mississippi that will be a model for the world of how people of differeent ethnic backgrounds can work together in harmony and peace. . . .

That was about it. The rest of my statement dealt with the need for an interstate highway in northeast Mississippi; the need for new and better paying jobs; for a fairer sales tax; for statewide health programs, particularly in the area of prenatal care; and for full support for Mississippi State University.

When I issued my first position paper in that campaign, I repeated the concerns I had listed above and included several other ones besides: compulsory school attendance through junior high school, improved public schools, state-approved day-care centers, licensed nursing homes in every county where there was a hospital, pollution control, consumer protection, and inducements for youth to remain in the state.

Later in that same campaign I issued position papers on

individual issues cited in my first public pronouncement. For example, I issued a paper on Mississippi highways. I pointed out that the available system of two-lane roads was dangerous and outdated—for medical patients, students, industry, and tourism. I pointed out the need for an interstate highway through northeast Mississippi from Meridian to the Tennessee line. I also said I believed there was a need for at least one east-west interstate highway through the area (meaning, of course, a widened Highway 82 which, as a two-lane highway, runs through Columbus through Starkville into the Delta and out of the state). In 1972, I pointed out, the federal government would be approving a federal interstate highway program. If Mississippi had a plan, Mississippi would get its share of these funds. After 1972, I warned, transportation dollars would increasingly be assigned to urban needs, so our rural area had to move quickly to get its share. I promised, if elected, to work hard for the highway needs of our area. I ended on what I hoped would be an attention-getting note: "The useless slaughter of people on broken-down two-lane highways must be stopped."

I repeated these and similar position papers in later campaigns, and they seemed to receive a good reception both from whites and from blacks. It was clear from the start that some whites would not vote for me under any circumstances simply because I was black. Some others, however, seemingly applauded my candidacy, promising me their votes. Indeed, some of them kept their promises. A number told me that they had voted for me specifically because they opposed my opponents. Most whites, however, voted for my opponents; in the early 1970s the memory of the boycott and integration activities I will discuss in the next two chapters was still too fresh.

I lost soundly every time I ran. In 1971, after my Inde-

pendent race for state senator from the Oktibbeha–
Noxubee County district was over, the local newspaper
said I had made the best showing of any of the Independent candidates that year. Still, I lost 8,427 to 4,219. In
Oktibbeha County, I lost 5,950 to 2,769. I have no way of
knowing how many whites voted for me or how many
blacks did not. If my 2,769 vote figure is matched against
the July 1971 list of 3,075 registered black voters, my total
is encouraging. However, some 1,400 voters were added
to the voting rolls between July and November. I have no
way of knowing how many of these new registrants were
black, but if 30 percent to 50 percent were, then there were
an additional 420 to 700 black voters on the rolls in
November. If every one of my 2,769 votes came from
black voters (which they did not), then approximately 700
to 1,000 blacks either did not vote for me or else stayed at
home.

When I ran for Starkville alderman in 1973, I lost again,
but it took my opponent two elections to gain the necessary majority. I lost in the runoff: 1,526 to 924. In 1975,
when I ran for the state legislature from Oktibbeha and
Noxubee counties, I lost Oktibbeha County 5,733 to
3,374, but carried 66 percent black Noxubee County 2,209
to 1,852.

Despite losing, I believe I made some progress each
time. I do not know the number of blacks and whites
registered in the 1973 and 1975 races, but I do know that
the black electorate increased and that I also gained more
white voters each time. Still, a black candidate could not
win in Oktibbeha County unless he or she ran from a
district which had a back majority. Tyrone Ellis has been
elected to the Mississippi legislature from a predominantly
black district. Other black officeholders in the county have
been successful wherever there have been enough black

133

voters to elect them. I never won, but I think I helped spotlight the race issue and allow others who followed me to be successful.

Each time I was, of course, disappointed at losing. What bothered me the most were the black voters who did not come out and vote for me, or who went to the polls and voted for my opponents. Most blacks supported my candidacies, but there were those who did not. I had no vocal opposition from any individuals, nor was there any factionalism in the black community against me. As far as I know, no black voter bore me any animosity.

Those blacks who did not vote for me took their positions for a variety of reasons. Some felt that no black had a chance to get elected, that my running was simply a waste of time, and so stayed away from the polls or voted for a white man whom they thought *could* win. Others worried that I *might* win. They feared I would then desert my practice. Cleverly, several of my opponents fanned this fear and conducted a "keep our black physician" campaign.

A number of other blacks did not vote for me out of fear of reprisals. Economic pressure was applied to keep them from supporting me. In one area of Oktibbeha County, for example, most blacks lived on plantations and worked for white landowners. These blacks were openly told not to vote for me because, if I won, they would lose their jobs.

Taking all these things into consideration, I believe I did well among black voters. Had I not been a doctor, had the black population been larger, had blacks been more accustomed to seeing black candidates, had there been no economic pressure, and had racial prejudice not kept more whites from voting for me, I might have been elected.

But I was not. I lost the three times I ran for office. Still, I enjoyed each experience, I learned something every time, and I believe I benefitted my community by making the efforts. However, I decided after the 1975 campaign that I would never run for elective office again. I am convinced that as long as I am a practicing physician I have no chance of winning. Looking back on the whole matter today, I often think that the voters may very well have been right in not electing me. Elective office would have taken time from my first love, medicine; perhaps it all worked out for the best.

Despite my defeats on the local level, I have continued to participate in politics. Local elections are not conducted under party labels, but I always participate as a concerned citizen. I try to take a stand on every issue and on every race that takes place in the county or in Starkville. I use one yardstick: is this candidate fair to all people or is he prejudiced against blacks? After deciding the answer to this question, I then try to jell the black vote behind the candidate who is most likely to be fair. I also try to back or oppose issues on the same basis. For example, I strongly opposed a 1978 county bond issue to build a jail in the Industrial Park section of the city because my concern over harsh police treatment of black prisoners convinced me that a jail in an isolated area would only make this circumstance worse. On the other hand, I supported a bond issue that same year for improving the Industrial Park and one in 1982 for expanding the hospital.

The local white power structure sees me as the major spokesman for the black community. I am regularly consulted by leaders from all sectors of the community. Usually this is done behind the scenes because local leaders are not overly anxious to be publicly identified with me. Federal officials also consult me. In 1980, for example, federal election officials were considering sending election monitors into several local counties. They asked my opinion, and I told them monitors had been necessary from the passage of the 1965 Voting Rights Act to about 1972, but not then. Blacks no longer were kept from the polls as they once had been. We no longer felt the need for federal presence at voting time.

Since I am constantly asked for advice, I keep my finger on the black community's pulse—either through my NAACP activities or through my medical practice. Blacks look to me for help and advice. I often receive phone calls in my office or at home, or I'm stopped on the street. "I'm in trouble," the speaker will say, "the mean white folks have done this or that to me. What can you do?" Or, while I am treating an individual for an ailment, he or she will sometimes want to talk more about matters of community concern than about what's ailing them. I believe I have a pretty good insight into black community attitudes, and blacks view me as a leader. Still, neither I nor anyone else can ever speak for every black person everywhere. There are just too many divergent black attitudes on every issue to be represented in one statement or opinion.

My real contribution, I believe, is not in expressing some nonexistent unified black community attitude on a specific issue but in giving the questioner my honest evaluation of the situation. Some members of the black community still cannot speak openly to whites on controversial issues. They tell a white person what he or she would like to hear rather than what the situation actually is. I always try to tell it as I see it and not as I think a white leader would like to hear it.

It has never been in my nature to be a militant, nor am I an Uncle Tom. I place myself somewhere to the left of center. I always try to portray a situation accurately, but to do it in a nice way; I try to tell it without vindictiveness. I always try to deal with issues and not with personalities. Should the Grand Dragon of the Ku Klux Klan, for example, spout off some of his ideas in my presence, I would firmly oppose what he said, but I would not attack him as a person. I try to deal with everyone that same way. Consequently, my relationship with the white power structure remains pleasant, even though I often say things its leaders do not want to hear.

I also try to be of service to my city and to my state by belonging to community organizations and accepting appointments to state and local boards and agencies. Once integration finally arrived in Starkville and in Mississippi in the 1970s, I became heavily involved in this kind of activity. I believe it is important to have black representation in all segments of the community and state, if black community needs are to be met. Therefore, I devote a great deal of time to civic participation. I also maintain membership in several all-black organizations like the Second Baptist Church, a black American Legion post, and a black Masonic order.

I spend most of my time in biracial organizations. I appear on panels at Mississippi State University, in the local schools, on local television, and in other forums where I might be able to provide a black perspective on some state or community issue. For example, during a referendum in the early 1980s on whether Starkville should allow the sale of beer, I appeared on a panel and represented both the black and the medical communities. When Mississippi State University had to hire a new football coach in the late 1970s, I was a member of the Search Committee.

A majority of my time, of course, is spent at the Oktibbeha County Hospital. I have never served as hospital chief of staff, but I have been staff secretary. I regularly attend staff meetings and the in-service training the hospital provides. Today, I am a member of the hospital's Pharmacy and Therapeutics Committee and the Medical Records Committee.

In addition, I am active in the local Chamber of Commerce and have served on a number of its committees over the years. In 1985, for example, I am a member of the Education Committee. As a member of the Chamber, I have a chance to exchange ideas with the community's business leaders on a regular basis, and to express to them black concerns. Unfortunately there are only a few black members. Too many blacks still see the Chamber as representative only of the white power structure, and therefore refuse to join. Others are not sure they would be welcome if they did. It will take special efforts to change these attitudes. Though the Chamber does not discriminate, it has as yet not made any special efforts to recruit black members. Consequently, my membership is important. As one of the few black members, I provide the little direct insight the Chamber has available to it on local black attitudes.

As a spin-off from my Chamber of Commerce membership, I have long served as a director of the Starkville Industrial Development Foundation, the group that oversees the city's Industrial Park. The task of the foundation during my term ending in 1983 was to encourage small pollution-free industry to locate in Starkville's Industrial Park area. Since an important part of the work force of any industry in Starkville is black, my directorship on the Foundation has been important to both the white and the black communities.

I have also been a member of several appointive committees and groups. From 1980 until it was merged with another sub-area in 1983, I was chairman of the Golden Triangle Sub-area Advisory Council to the Mississippi Health Services Agency, a federally mandated committee whose purpose was to ensure the most efficient use of federal funds for medical facilities in the state. The council's task was to approve or disapprove any medical construction in the Golden Triangle region in order to prevent unnecessary duplication. Similarly, from 1980 to 1984, I was a member of the Mississippi State Block Grant Committee, an advisory group to the governor on the allocation of federal funds. From 1977 to 1979 I was chairman of the board of the Prairie Minority Small Business Enterprise, an outgrowth of a federal program to encourage the development of small businesses among minority groups. Our task was to help provide training and other support for individuals trying to establish small businesses or to help those already in existence.

Finally, in 1977, I became a member of the board of directors of a new bank in Starkville, The Bank of North Mississippi. As one of the stockholders and a director of this institution, I regularly meet with the rest of the board to set policy and approve major loans. I have been told I am the first black person to serve as a bank director in the state, and perhaps this is true. In any case, my involvement in this bank provides a black face in another place where normally society does not expect to see one.

Looking back on my participation in civic and political affairs, I continue to believe that people's involvement is necessary if society is to improve. Some of my medical colleagues say that politics is dirty and cheap and that it is beneath me to deal with it. I disagree with this attitude wholeheartedly, and believe that unless we can ensure the election of the right kind of people to public office our country will deteriorate. Even from a selfish vantage point, it is important for me to participate. What is bad for the country as a whole will usually be bad for me as an individual. It is advantageous for all of us to make sure that good, decent people are elected to office and that meaningful laws are passed and meaningful programs espoused. Only in this way can society be improved for everyone's betterment.

I also believe that government, at all levels, should continue to play an important role in American society. I do not believe that government should be the great father and hand out everything to everybody, but I feel it ought to ensure that all citizens have an equal opportunity to reach their full potential. If, for example, there is a bright student who wants to become a chemist but cannot afford the necessary education, the government should make the funds available to him or her. Every ablebodied American ought to be able to earn his or her own way; but it is the government's job to make sure that he or she has every chance to do so. And it is up to all American citizens to participate in politics to ensure that the government does its job.

As a black man I have felt an even stronger pull toward the political arena because of my sense of obligation to the black community. The only difference between my participation in politics and that of my white counterparts has been my background and my experience with being black in American society. I think I would be in politics were I white. Because I am black, however, my political involvement has been a crusade to try to make sure that equal opportunities are always open to blacks. My involvement in politics is another part of my human rights beliefs and my medical oath. Wherever I see hurt, I want to be able to heal it. Medicine is the great healer of physical ills; politics can be the great healer of social ills. I see myself as a physician in both spheres.

Mississippi has come a long way since the days of my youth. It is hardly a racial paradise, but it is certainly not the kind of place I remember as a child in Hattiesburg during the 1920s and 1930s—or even the kind of place I recall as a beginning physician in Starkville in the 1950s. Today, blacks are an integral part of the state, and we are treated with a respect unheard of before. As a child I heard my elders bemoan their political exclusion. They would not even think of voting, running for office, or holding positions in the state party. I have done all of these things. We have come a long way, despite the distance we have yet to travel.

9
HUMAN RIGHTS—
THE SCHOOLS

Throughout the late 1960s and 1970s, and into the 1980s I remained involved in politics at the local and state level. I hope I contributed to the progress we have made in this area. During this same time I continued my busy medical practice, seeing patients and working to keep up with the continuing changes in medical science. In the Starkville area, the late 1960s and early 1970s saw three events take place that resulted in fundamental changes in our community. Mississippi State University admitted its first black student, the Starkville public schools were integrated, and economic opportunities for blacks were improved. I have left these topics for the final chapters because, although they were happening at the same time as my political involvement, I believe they could only have happened in the wake of the many political changes I have already discussed.

I have mentioned the tightly segregated nature of Starkville and Mississippi State University. Neither city nor school showed any disposition to change its segregationist policies, both remaining silent as the civil rights movement sent barriers crashing down all over the state. Still, it was at the university that the first dramatic integration breakthrough in the Starkville area took place.

In 1962 violence accompanying the admission of the

first black student at the University of Mississippi shocked the nation. The following year the Mississippi State basketball Bulldogs won the Southeastern Conference title and gained an automatic bid to the NCAA basketball championship tournament, but there was an unwritten rule that Mississippi athletic teams did not play opponents who had any black players. In this case, Mississippi State's opponent in the first round was to be Loyola University of Chicago, a school whose starting team was predominantly black. President D. W. Colvard decided that the Bulldogs would play Loyola, and despite some serious opposition, the team left Mississippi to compete. Loyola beat the Bulldogs on its way to a national championship, but what was more important than the game was the destruction of a major color barrier.

In 1965 the college itself was integrated. My adopted son, Richard Holmes, became the first black student at that institution by enrolling in the second summer session of 1965.

My involvement in the integration of Mississippi State had begun, I suppose, some nine years earlier. One of my patients in the mid-1950s was a lady named Eliza Hunter who lived on North Washington Street with several grandchildren. Mrs. Hunter developed cancer of the breast, and, by the time she sought my help the cancer had grown so large that it was inoperable. My treatment was palliative; I gave her medicine to control the pain. I also visited her regularly at her home, and we got to know each other quite well.

Mrs. Hunter knew she was dying, and she worried about her youngest grandchild, twelve-year-old Richard. One day she looked at me and said, "I feel pretty secure except for my little boy here. I'm kind of worried about him. I know I'm going to go off the scene in a little while. When I do, I want you to take him into your house and rear him up. He's got some parents, but they don't care nothin' about him." I already knew Richard, and we had developed a close relationship. Even before I began taking care of his grandmother, he had come around to my office. "I need a job, Doc," he said. I started him with odd jobs like sweeping the floor, and he became quite a fixture around the office. So, when his grandmother asked me to take him, I said I would.

My wife and young daughters knew Richard and liked him, but they were not all that sure that adopting him was a good idea. The more we talked about it, however, the more the idea appealed to us. We began to see him as the son and brother we had always wanted. Richard joined our family and quickly became an older brother to my daughters and a son to me and my wife. It was almost impossible to dislike him. He was willing to do anything asked of him. (He never changed his name only because he wanted to maintain some identity with his family of birth.)

When it was time for Richard to begin college, he chose Wiley College, a small black school in Texas. He liked the school, made many friends there, and was doing well scholastically. About this same time in 1962, James Meredith was making history by integrating the University of Mississippi. Richard was, of course, aware of the Meredith incident, but he had no desire to join him at Ole Miss or to attend any other white school. Richard simply wanted to get an education and become a doctor.

When he came home in the summer of 1965, he decided to take a couple of nonscience courses in summer school, so that he could concentrate on his science curriculum when he returned to Wiley in the fall. He first applied to Alcorn and Jackson State, two black state institutions. Then he decided this made no sense. Why should he have to incur the additional expense and trouble of going somewhere else when there was a college in his own home-town? He decided to apply to Mississippi State, not to integrate it but to be close to home while he took courses that summer. He asked me what I thought, and I said I would support him. That was about it. There was no grand plotting or planning. Richard decided to go to Mississippi State simply because it was convenient.

Richard wrote ahead early in the summer to begin the registration process. I heard that when the school received his letter there were many meetings and much scuffling around in response. The Meredith example at Ole Miss loomed large in the minds of Mississippi State officials. Everyone from the president down was determined that Mississippi State would not experience the same turmoil and bloodshed that Ole Miss had. Besides, the school depended heavily on federal funds and could not afford to jeopardize this money by tolerating anti-integration violence.

Registration day arrived, and all was in readiness. The school had arranged for a heavy police presence, and I had spoken to the county sheriff, who promised his cooperation. That morning our whole family felt the tension, but everyone was calm. My wife, the typical mother, was apprehensive, but calmly told Richard not to get upset at anything that might happen. I drove Richard out to the campus, my mind swimming with all kinds of thoughts. I too felt concern, but I also felt confident. My conversations and investigations had convinced me that the school had worked hard to ensure him a peaceful welcome. As we drove, we said little of substance. Richard seemed composed and spoke of his desire for an education and his hope all would go well. I dropped him off in front of the Animal Husbandry Building where he was to register at 2 P.M. As he got out of the car, the only advice I gave him was: "Keep your head up." He nodded in return. I drove back

145

to my office to wait for his call, so I could pick him up. I tried not to worry much.

Richard called me in several hours, and I went out to get him. He told me he had encountered no difficulties. Practically no one paid any attention to him, and only the presence of the extra policemen indicated that something unusual was happening. He received some stares while registering and while walking across campus to Lee Hall to pay his fees. A few students he knew spoke to him as he passed by. He told a brief news conference the school had arranged that he was there because State was near his home and was highly rated. He was not there for any fanfare or publicity. That was about it. The first black student had peacefully registered at Mississippi State University.

Unfortunately the calm was soon broken. The following evening about two hundred students gathered at the campus and moved down Gillespie Street. They marched to our home and circled it, shouting racial insults. We stayed inside, obviously frightened, but determined not to provoke any unnecessary violence. We kept all the outside lights on, and could see that, despite the shouting, the mob was doing no damage to our house or property. I waited as long as I could before calling the police, and the mob left before they arrived. The students marched back to campus, having apparently vented their spleen. Actually, I believe the mob consisted of more than students; some riffraff had joined in. But the whole thing did start on the campus. Whatever the case, that was the only problem my family or I ever had. After that, there were no further marches.

Richard had no difficulties in class or on campus that summer, but he did experience the tactic of silent rejection. He was simply ignored. A few students were outwardly hostile, but even fewer made any effort to be friendly. It was apparently not socially acceptable to welcome the school's first black student.

Richard did well in his psychology and government classes that summer and began preparing to return to Wiley in the fall. This time I stepped in. After discussing the matter with other black community leaders, I asked Richard to consider transferring from Wiley permanently. I was afraid that if he did not stay at Mississippi State no other black student would ever enter the school. There was another young man in Starkville who wanted to go to State, but he said he would not go there alone. I urged Richard to stay. He thought about it and decided to transfer permanently.

Fall registration was also uneventful. With the full student body present, however, Richard felt more animosity. Again, there was no physical violence, but the catcalls and insults increased. No one ever insulted him to his face, however; the insults were usually hurled from a distance. He continued to be isolated. When he sat down at a library table, everyone else left. When he entered a TV lounge, it quickly emptied. But, all in all, these things were minor. Over and over Richard heard people at the school say: "We don't want the same thing to happen here that happened at Ole Miss." Consequently, most people bent over backwards to make his stay as pleasant as possible.

Since that time Richard has continued to be very successful. After teaching in Alabama and spending two years in the army as a paratrooper and military police investigator, he earned a master's degree at Mississippi State with additional hours in science. He then proceeded to Michigan State University, where he graduated from medical school in 1977. He interned at the University of Alabama Medical School's Family Practice Center in Tuscaloosa and afterward completed a two-year emergency

147

medicine residency in Toledo, Ohio. Today, he is an emergency room physician in Alabaster, Alabama, in the Birmingham area. He is married and has a young daughter and a young son.

The integration of the university had little impact on black-white relations in Starkville. In town, life remained segregated. There was very little antiblack violence; it was simply a matter of two worlds totally apart. Blacks were subordinated to the dominant white society.

The example of all the civil rights activities in other parts of the state, the passage of the federal Civil Rights and Voting Rights acts, and the local voter registration experience, all began to create a climate in Starkville favorable for more action. Still, it was an uphill battle. Many blacks were so subordinated that they could not even imagine battling the system. The attitude was: "Let's wait and see what the good white people are going to do. They'll do what's right. They'll do what they're supposed to do."

Even those willing to take a stand had to consider the consequences. Blacks were not supposed to speak out except in praise of the status quo. There was little use of violence, but the threat of loss of employment was often enough to silence any would-be critic. I remember well, for example, how schoolteachers were asked whether they belonged to the NAACP and threatened with firing if they did.

Beneath the quiet surface, however, things were starting to happen. On April 1, 1969, we met at the Griffin Methodist Church to organize the Oktibbeha County chapter of the NAACP. I made the keynote speech. I had tried to get Aaron Henry or Charles Evers to come, but both men were so busy they could not make it. I attempted to deal with the local inertia myself. I told the packed church that the whole matter came down to us in

148

the Oktibbeha County area speaking out "as one large, united, dynamic, courageous whole." We had to resolve never again to permit or tolerate injustice, and to use "every legal means to fight it."

> Be it selective buying, defeat at the polls, marches, sit ins, legal suits, or other legal means. We are tired of being second class citizens! We are tired of being the last hired and the first fired! We are tired of our children and grandchildren going to 2nd and 3rd class schools! We are tired of all the white collar jobs being held by whites! We are tired of being cheated, robbed, beaten and humiliated! We are tired of grinning and bearing it.

And then I tried to confront the foot-draggers in the black community:

> To those among us who think that white is always right—the Uncle Toms, Uncle Remuses, the Aunt Jemimas and all of the brain washed Blacks—we admonish you now to get out of our way—to step aside—to make way for proud Blacks who are not ashamed of their race or color—to make way for the new spirit of Black Pride, Black Power and Black Awareness that will one day make us Free!

This meeting to establish our local chapter of the NAACP took place because blacks had finally become convinced that the NAACP was indeed needed. Starkville blacks had slowly begun to realize that something had to be done.

A major target of black community concern was the segregated school system in the city and the county. As early as 1954 the United States Supreme Court had issued its *Brown v. Board of Education* school integration decsion. The bloody integration of the University of Mississippi had taken place in 1962. In 1965, as I have already indicated, my adopted son integrated Mississippi State University peacefully. All over the South, barrier after barrier had fallen before the onslaught of Martin Luther King, the Southern Christian Leadership Conference, and a host of other civil rights individuals and organizations. Yet in the late 1960s the Starkville and Oktibbeha County public schools were still segregated.

The situation was even more distressing because Starkville had been forced to begin thinking of integration as early as 1965. That year the school district had to submit to the United States Office of Education a desegregation plan. That federal government agency had promptly rejected the plan as inadequate, and for the next five years letters between Washington and Starkville were frequent. The federal government tried to get the city to integrate its schools (to end the dual system, as the expression was in those days), while the school board tried to do as little as possible to comply. On July 16, 1965, the board devised what was to be its basic position for the next five years: a freedom-of-choice plan to provide minimal integration. This first plan called for students to have freedom of choice as to which of the schools they attended. A timetable was established as follows: 1965–66: freedom of choice for students in grades, 1, 2, 3, and 12; 1966–68, freedom of choice for students in grades 1–6 and 11–12; 1967–68: freedom of choice for all students.

The school district operated under this system for the next several years, and, not surprisingly, the dual system remained intact. Whites did not ask to attend black schools, and most black students were too frightened or intimidated to try to attend the all-white schools. From April 1966 through June 1967 the United States Office of Education tried to get more faculty and student integration, but school district officials insisted that they were doing all they could, considering the situation in Starkville.

In August 1967 three representatives of the Equal Opportunities Section of the United States Office of Education came to Starkville, looked the situation over, and reported that integration progress there was not satisfactory. The federal government then threatened to cut off all federal funds, and the school board promised to work on a new long-range plan. The board submitted several faculty desegregation plans to Washington, but federal officials were not impressed with any of them and began efforts to cut off funds. Three long-range student integration plans then made their way to Washington in 1968, but again all three were rejected. On September 13, 1968, the federal government cut off funds to the school district. (That academic year, only 80 of approximately 1,600 black students in the system attended white schools. No whites attended the black schools. Such was Starkville integration.)

Throughout this period blacks kept hoping that the white establishment would do what was right. When the school board continued operating the schools under the freedom of choice plan which the federal government had rejected so dramatically, this was the last straw. We realized that only legal action would ever end the dual system in Starkville. On July 2, 1968, I helped organize some twenty blacks in the city and thirty others in the county to go to the United States District Court for the Northern District, Eastern Division, in Aberdeen, Mississippi, to ask for a court-ordered end to the dual system.

It took a year for our suit to rise to the top of the jammed docket of the federal court. Judge Orma Smith was not able to hold a hearing until August 5, 1969, but the following day he issued an order giving Starkville until

December 1, 1969, to provide a two-year plan to end the dual system. After much public and behind-the-scenes activity on the part of the school board, concerned whites of all persuasions, and worried blacks, the school board submitted a plan to continue freedom of choice in 1970–71 and then in 1971–72 establish integrated school zones for grades 1–6 and an integrated junior high and an integrated high school for grades 7–12. Obvious in the plan was the fact that all the former black schools, except one, were to be closed. (A school district poll had indicated that Starkville whites did not want their children to attend classes in formerly black school buildings.) The Starkville plan also called for the continued admission of some four hundred county students into the city schools. Ominous, too, was the establishment of standards for the retention of teachers, standards that blacks feared were meant to eliminate or at best reduce black professionals in a unitary system. The court order allowed those of us who were plaintiffs in the case to indicate our reactions to the school board plan, and we protested vigorously in early January 1970. The board then submitted another plan based on recommendations of a biracial committee of which I was part. Even this plan did not use the former black school buildings as effectively as I thought possible, so I opposed it.

Judge Smith held another hearing on February 5, 1970. Two days later he issued his order. Beginning with the 1970–71 school year, the dual system was to be abolished. All the existing school buildings, former black and former white schools, were to be used. All the city's first and second graders were to attend a former all-white school, third graders were to attend a former black school, fourth graders a former black school, fifth graders a former white school, and so on. Judge Smith ordered immediate faculty desegragation, and ordered that there was to be no discrimination either in busing or in any other school activities.

The judge also institutionalized the already existing biracial committee, which had worked especially hard all through January to try to deal with the situation. I and others participated in meetings where an attempt was made to reach a biracial position on school uses. On this committee, professors associated with Mississippi State University spearheaded the white community participation. Their major concern was the continuation of the public school system in Starkville; they were afraid that if whites pulled their children out of the public schools and established an academy, integration would fail there as it had failed in some other Mississippi communities. They worked for integration for the good of their children, as those of us who are black worked for the good of our children. We did not always agree on the best approach, but the fact that we met regularly opened channels of communication which were not otherwise available. In December 1969 a group of whites had published in the local newspaper a petition of support for the public schools signed by more than a thousand people. The establishment of the Tombigbee Human Relations Council by Donna Meyer was also important. This goodwill proved very significant when integration came in February 1970.

Thinking over the whole issue some fifteen years later, I find it difficult to keep all the facts clear in my mind. The whole matter was very complex, and, except for the fact that legal documentation from that period has been preserved by the federal court, I would not be able to recall even the little I have mentioned here. While I was trying to deal with school integration, there was also the matter of a boycott of the business district, voting rights, Democratic politics, and, most of all, my medical practice. All these

153

things were going on at the same time, and they have blurred together in my mind. There were many blacks and many whites who played important roles in the coming of integration, but I will not mention any here for fear of leaving someone out. There were friendships lost and animosities developed, but the job was done. The dual system was eliminated; sixteen years after the Supreme Court ruled segregated schools unconstitutional, Starkville was finally in compliance. It had been a long fight, but it was worth it.

The 1970s were hardly a racial paradise in the Starkville school system. I was pleased to see children from both races begin to attend school together in the fall of 1970 without any violence or major difficulties. This was most encouraging. Yet everything did not go as well as I would have liked. One of the immediate results of integration was a cutback in black principals and teachers. I do not remember anyone getting fired outright in that first year of integration, although several years later two white teachers lost their jobs because they differed with some school district policy. They had to go to federal court to seek damages, and they won. Blacks lost their representation in the teaching and administrative staffs by attrition. Of the three black principles at the time of integration, one retired and one took a job in another district. Fenton Peters alone retained a principalship. Among the teachers, a few retired, a few took other jobs, and some were forced to teach out of their area of competence. (In 1985, there are three black principals, a black central office administrator, and a black school board member. There are still fewer black teachers than I would like.)

My own wife was one of the casualties of school integration. Nita taught for only two months in the integrated system. She had a class that was about fifty/fifty black and

154

white. One day the white principal came to her because one of the white students in her class had received a low test grade. "Do you know whose child this is?" he asked. "This is Mr. So and So's child. She can't make a grade like that." "Oh yes, she can, "my wife said. "She did, and that's the grade she gets." The discussion became very heated after this, and my wife finally had enough and quit on the spot. She did not teach the rest of the term, and the following year she took a position in the county school system.

At first, then, the black professional did not benefit from the coming of integration, but the black children seemed to be treated fairly; there was no resegregation of the races inside the schools. In following years, however, the use of achievement tests resegregated children according to standarized score groupings. All-black and all-white classes began to appear. As late as the early 1980s our local NAACP chapter had to take action with the Civil Rights Division of the Justice Department to prevent this kind of tracking from continuing. In 1985, we are again in federal court to try to eliminate tracking and require the hiring of more black faculty members.

Some whites, as I have indicated, worked hard for integration, and they played important roles in bringing it about. Others, however, were ambivalent at best. The general white attitude seemed to be: "Integration is something we don't want, but the big bad federal government is forcing it on us, so we have to comply." The federal government was a convenient scapegoat for many whites to justify their acceptance of integration. But at least they accepted it.

There were others, however, who refused to accept the inevitable. Rather than send their children to integrated schools, they banded together to form the local academy.

Stockholders of the Citizens Realty, Inc. donated ten acres to a hastily formed Oktibbeha Educational Foundation. The three major banks at that time contributed sums of money, while other individuals provided financial aid less conspicuously. Obviously, all these people were well within their rights, and I do not argue otherwise.

I have heard all the justifications for the all-white academy: that it took all the confirmed segregationists out of the public school system and allowed peaceful integration; that the academy exists for people living in the county areas where education is supposedly inferior; that the academy does not threaten Starkville's good public school system; that the academy fulfills a need for the class conscious—that it is snobbishness, not race that explains its existence. I have heard all these and other arguments, but none of them makes any sense to me.

To my way of thinking, blatant racism was the reason for the etablishment of the academy in Starkville. The argument at the time was not very subtle: "The schools will be mixed now. Pretty soon black boys will be chasing after and marrying white girls." Apparently the argument was rather successful because when the institution opened there were numerous parents who left their boys in public schools and sent their girls to the academy. Yes, I believe snobbishness plays a role in explaining the existence of the academy in our city, as do any number of other reasons. But I am convinced that race is the major reason. Without the coming of integration, there would not have been nor would there be an academy in Starkville today.

The academy is a real sore spot with me. I see it as a threat to public education. It is a constant reminder to both whites and blacks that there is much more to do before the races are truly brought together. Fortunately the Starkville public schools are thoroughly integrated. While they are not free from problems one might expect in any school system, the vast majority of whites and blacks in the community support them. The city's academy has a limited clientele and a limited influence, but I find its very existence repugnant to all I believe in and hope for. Blacks as a whole are disappointed that it exists.

10

HUMAN RIGHTS—ECONOMIC ISSUES

Once integration came to the university and to the public schools, black problems in Starkville did not end. Blacks were still suffering from economic difficulties. There was common agreement in the black community of the need to improve employment opportunities, and this usually led to a discussion of the absence of black salespersons in downtown stores. On all Main Street there was only one black salesperson, and that was a black woman at Kleban's Shoe Store. Blacks worked downtown as janitors, cleaning ladies, and in other menial capacities, but that was about the extent of it. For a long time people had been saying that something had to be done. Finally we decided to act.

In February 1970 I called the first meeting of what at first we called the Oktibbeha County Black Caucus to discuss the matter formally. We were a very small group, about eight or ten people: Bennie Butler, the barber; undertaker W. B. Robinson; Clarence Taylor, a pool hall owner; John McGhee, a laborer at the university; and Thomas Brooks, a carpenter, to mention a few. After a while a whole stream of other people came in. Neither the local nor the state NAACP participated for fear of legal reprisals. We decided to approach local business leaders, point out the lack of black salespeople in their stores, and work with them to hire some.

Our initial efforts to try to talk with the store owners as a group failed. They refused to meet with us. So we sent delegations to each of them, one by one, presented our grievances, and asked them to hire blacks in their stores. One by one they told us no. They were not hostile; they were not sympathetic; they were simply noncommittal. Their first reaction to our call for more black employment was usually to say that they already had a black janitor or that they did not need any more black cleanup help. When we told them we wanted salespersons, not janitors, they refused. Their excuse was always the same: "If we hire blacks as salespeople, we will lose our white trade." We countered with the argument that they also had a substantial black trade, and they might lose this if they did not act. That argument had no effect. They stood their ground. A March 1970 meeting with the Chamber of Commerce was similarly nonproductive.

Our next action was to approach city officials in April of that year and ask them to encourage the merchants to hire blacks. At the same time, we said that city and county government also needed blacks in meaningful positions. The mayor and the city fathers listened, but they too were noncommittal. They told us they had no leverage with the merchants; there was nothing they could do. The merchants would have to make up their own minds. As for blacks in government, again they insisted they could do nothing. The only way blacks could hold any meaningful government offices was to get themselves elected. No mention was made of the obvious number of nonelected people working for local government who had always been white but could just as well be black.

Obviously we had arrived at a standstill. We had tried to

159

reason with the white leadership of Starkville, and we had been unsuccessful, so we decided on a boycott. We made up a list of stores where blacks regularly shopped and announced we would encourage the black community to boycott them until they hired black help. In our early planning we talked about boycotting all the merchants at once, but we immediately realized this would be impossible. Blacks could simply not afford to go to Columbus or West Point to shop, so we had to leave some places open in Starkville for them to buy needed goods. For example, we boycotted a grocery store on Main Street because about that time a black man had opened a grocery where blacks could go instead. Usually, though, unboycotted stores for black use were white-owned.

We began the boycott by announcing it in the local churches one Sunday morning in late April. We had some leaflets printed up explaining our tactics. The black community reaction was wholeheartedly positive. Blacks from early childhood to senior adulthood were organized to march up and down the Main Street sidewalks. These pickets carried signs like "No Black Sales People, No Business" and "Blacks Should Be Treated Fairly."

When we decided on boycott action to force the merchants to act, we looked for expert help. (Up to this point, we had had none.) Someone mentioned that a man named R. B. Cotton-Reader, a professional organizer, lived in nearby Grenada. He had marched with Martin Luther King and had gained a great deal of experience with the kind of action we were planning. He was a determined, outgoing individual, so we asked him to come to Starkville and organize our effort. He agreed and became the mastermind of the boycott from that point on, the only outsider involved.

We did not have a lot of money to pay Cotton-Reader, but, fortunately, he agreed to work with us if we provided living quarters and the cost of his food and other expenses. Throughout the boycott we held drives and fish fries to raise funds; the churches contributed a little money; and some of us chipped in from our own pockets. The money we raised provided the funds to purchase a house trailer for Cotton-Reader out in the county on Old West Point Road.

Cotton-Reader was here for several months and furnished the necessary expertise to keep the boycott going. A number of us provided local leadership, but Cotton-Reader's association with Martin Luther King gave him the status to attract widespread support for the movement. I doubt whether I or anyone else in Starkville could have rallied people the way he did. His leadership abilities, but mostly the mystique of his connection with Martin Luther King, made him the effective organizer he was.

Once Cotton-Reader arrived, the movement fell into a normal pattern. Every night members of the Black Caucus met with him to plan strategy for the following day. He would make suggestions; we would discuss them; sometimes we would accept them; at other times we would alter them to fit the local situation. Normally we would have about ten pickets marching up and down the Main Street sidewalks, carrying signs. Then, there might be an afternoon protest march followed by a meeting explaining the philosophy and purpose of the boycott to be sure the black community understood precisely what was going on. Cotton-Reader conducted these meetings, and there and at the financial gatherings he encouraged and cajoled people to participate in the boycott and to do so nonviolently. Cotton-Reader was an effective organizer, and, except for some verbal harrassment from the police, he was generally left alone to do his work.

The white reaction to the boycott was as negative as the black reaction was positive. We did have some sympathetic onlookers, but few whites actually participated.

161

There was also no organized white opposition. Most of the time whites simply tried to discourage us. The local newspaper tried to ignore us, printing practically nothing about our activities. Quite a few people told me personally that the whole thing was a mistake. They made comments like: "You've got too much to lose. You've got it made; why bother with this sort of stuff?" On the picket line we received a much more hostile reaction. There was no direct violence, but picketers, especially the younger ones, were often hassled by passersby and became involved in some scuffles with them and with the police. Some store owners continually complained to the police about our activities and demanded that authorities keep us away from their stores.

The biggest source of conflict between us and the white community centered on the marches we conducted through the downtown area. At least once a week, and then two to three times a week during May and June 1970, we gathered at the Masonic Temple on North Washington Street and marched to the courthouse and back. Sometimes when we reached the courthouse we turned on to Main Street to parade through the entire business district. The tighter and more successful the boycott became and the more we marched, the more frustrated the merchants became. They put greater and greater pressure on the police to stop the marching. The police began to warn us that they would stop issuing us permits, but they always relented at the last minute.

In early June the city took its stand. One June 2 the Board of Aldermen passed two new ordinances, one to govern marches and the other to govern picketing. In order to march, permission was first required from the chief of police, who could deny a permit if changes he wanted in march plans were not made. On June 4, when we wanted to march, we were told: "There isn't going to be a march today." We replied: "There *is* going to be a march today." We gathered, 161 of us, at the Masonic Temple and began to move, double file, toward the Oktibbeha County courthouse, carefully observing traffic regulations and acting in an orderly manner. At a spot on Washington Street across from the courthouse we were all arrested for "obstructing public streets or sidewalks." We were not jailed, however, but were told to appear for trial on June 10. On June 6 we marched again, and again we were arrested and released. We were determined to march, and the city was determined to prevent us.

On June 9 we tried again. This time 180 of us gathered at the corner of Main and Jackson streets, in front of the Stark Hotel, and began marching west on Main. We passed the courthouse and started north on Washington Street when the chief of police stopped us about halfway between Main and Jefferson streets. He told us that since we had not been issued a permit, we had to break up or go to jail. I was one of several who were leading the march. The chief addressed me personally several times. "Doc, you can go back to work now. You don't have to do this. We're going to arrest you all if you go any further. Why don't you go, just go back to your patients?" We kept right on marching, and when we reached Jefferson Street near the county jail behind the courthouse, the police began arresting us for marching without a permit.

We had decided that, like Martin Luther King, we would be nonviolent throughout, so we accepted the arrest peacefully and there was no violence. All of us, young and old, male and female, Cotton-Reader, Starkville black leadership, and the rank and file were arrested. This time we were not released for trial. I and several others were put into the county jail downtown. Most of the marchers, including my oldest daughter, were bused to a storage building at the then black athletic field, today West Side

163

Park. The county jail was too small to hold everyone. Those at the athletic field building and those of us in the jail were all crowded and uncomfortable, but the storage building detainees had it the worst.

The march had begun right after mid-day dinner. We were arrested about the middle of the afternoon, and we stayed in jail for several days. The police continued to try to convince me to leave. "Doc, you just get up and go now. There won't be any charges or anything. Go back to your patients." I would not move. I said: "No, as long as the rest of them have to stay, I'm going to stay too." My daughter similarly refused to leave as long as anyone else was in jail. It was clear that the police hoped to get me to leave in order to discredit my leadership and cause the boycott to collapse. I was considered the major leader of the movement, and authorities believed if I left, that would end it. I stood my ground.

In jail we talked, sang freedom songs, and just passed the time. We refused to pay the $100 cash or the $500 property bail bond on principle and because many of the marchers simply were not financially able to do so. Instead we got a lawyer from neighboring West Point and that same day at 4:50 P.M. he filed a class-action suit against the city in the U.S. District Court in Aberdeen. We asked for a preliminary and a permanent injunction to keep the city from enforcing the ordinance and from using arrests "for the purpose of chilling and depriving" us of our constitutional rights. The next day our lawyers specifically asked for our release from jail because of "excessive bail as further punishment" for the exercise of our rights.

The city immediately called for a full hearing on the matter. The city attorney said we had "created near chaos" in the city during the last two weeks, citing the mayor's call for a curfew, the police force's 24-hour shifts, the shooting at a car, the uncertain liquid shot by water pistol into a transient's eye, the burning of an old wooden building at the Henderson school complex, the alleged spitting on and cursing of policemen, and the previous arrests. The city brief never specifically accused us of doing any of these things, but it said that if we won this case the result would be "chaos and riots" in Starkville.

Then the lawyer for the city tried to damage our case even more. He reminded the court of the recently issued court order desegregating the schools. This order enjoined me (whom he cited by name) and others involved in that case from entering the schools and, in general, from interfering with their operations. The lawyer insisted that our demonstrations, allegedly "seeking the lowering of the school standards and requirements as previously set by the courts" and demanding more black teachers, were in violation of the court order. This statement was so obviously ridiculous that the court never considered it.

The next day, June 11, the city submitted a document which detailed a list of alleged recent fire bombings in the city. Again, we were not specifically accused of these acts, but warned that Starkville was "on the brink of chaos."

Throughout all its statements, the city insisted that it was conducting itself legally and was not violating our rights. We had full freedom to practice our first-amendment privileges if only we would do it according to Mississippi law and the Starkville ordinance. The city lawyer told the court that police were acting properly to maintain law and order against our assaults on it.

Meanwhile, we were still in jail. On June 11, twenty-eight people tried to march again, but they were arrested and released on their own recognizance. At the same time, Judge Orma R. Smith held a hearing into the matter. He enjoined the city from requiring bond and ordered our release. He further enjoined the city from prosecuting us on any charges related to the case until after a June 23 hearing on our motion for an injunction. He also said we could not picket or march until after that same hearing.

We were happy to be let out of jail, though concerned about the judge's temporary ban on marching. We had our lawyers immediately ask for permission to march during the period before the hearing. On June 18 the judge issued such permission along with a series of do's and don'ts. Basically, the regulations resembled the city ordinance, but they did not give the chief of police the power to deny us march permission or require a permit tax. For our part, we had to tell the police chief of our plans one hour before we began.

On June 22 both we and the city accepted the parade guidelines, but when we marched the following day, the police harassed us with arrest threats because they said we were violating the agreement. It was difficult to maintain the exact required distance between marchers and groups of marchers, but the city seemed intent on considering such things as crucial. We tried our best to obey the entire agreement, but we did not believe "technical requirements" were as important as the city made them out to be.

On June 24 Judge Smith issued his final ruling. In sum, he said peaceful marches could take place in Starkville subject only to the agreed-upon guidelines. As long as these rules were followed and the rights of nonmarchers were respected, the city could not prohibit march and picket activity on public property. On July 29 both sides agreed to follow these guidelines, and on December 19, 1970, Judge Smith issued a jointly agreed-upon order of dismissal. The issue had been settled; constitutional rights had been ensured.

All this legal activity was time consuming and expensive. Meanwhile, we continued our boycott. Other than being arrested, being put in jail, and having to go to court, neither I nor anyone else suffered any real discomfort from our boycott or marching activities. We also did not receive any direct threats, though all kinds of rumors were always floating around. It was whispered one time that a local business leader was threatening to shoot me the next time we marched. He supposedly warned he just might get his gun, pick me out because I was taller than most of the marchers, and shoot my head off. I never heard any more of this alleged threat and never learned whether the person who relayed the warning to me had heard it right or not. Whatever the case, it did not deter me from marching, and nothing ever happened.

After a time the white merchants saw that the boycott was having an effect on their businesses, so they agreed to meet with us as a group. The meetings were loosely organized and sometimes became very hot. The merchants did not seem to have one definite spokesman, while Butler, Brooks, or I spoke for us. Cotton-Reader usually just sat and listened. As time went on, a significant change became obvious. When we had first begun talking to them, the merchants' response had been: "No, never." As the boycott progressed, their tone became: "What do you want of us? What do you want us to do?" We repeated over and over that we wanted black sales-people in their stores. We also wanted jobs for blacks in the city's factories, and, as a spinoff, we began insisting that there should be black policemen and black firemen. They listened but did not seem to hear.

The boycott continued while we met regularly with the white leadership. No new black faces appeared behind sales counters on Main Street. Even worse, black enthusiasm began to wane. The strong early support for the boycott began to deteriorate as the movement moved into the fall of 1970. Christmas was drawing near, and people began complaining that they just *had* to get such and such from this or that boycotted store. Some blacks began sneaking into these stores by the back door, and the white merchants, of course, encouraged them. Several times when I was picketing I saw a lady I knew enter a store by the back door. We sent some pickets to wait for her to come out, but she stayed in a very long time and got by us again.

We did not physically try to prevent anyone, black or white, from entering any store; our picketing was peaceful. When black persons like this lady shopped at a boycotted store, we announced the fact by word of mouth, hoping that such notoriety would deter similar action in the future. For a while it did, but, as Christmas drew closer, more and more of our support began to drift away through back doors. We knew we had to do something quickly, so we ended the boycott. We announced that the merchants had promised that they would hire blacks in their stores in return for our ending our movement. By this time the merchant position had evolved to the following attitude: "As long as you're threatening us, we're not going to do anything, but, if you stop this silly boycott, we'll start hiring some blacks." In fact, we had no firm promises, but we also had no other choice. We had to take the position that the merchants had agreed to our demands because the boycott would have come apart, no matter what we did.

Sometime later, black faces began to appear in Main Street stores. The irony of the whole thing was that some of those hired were individuals who had not participated in the boycott or had actually broken it by sneaking into stores when the pickets had not been looking. There was some dissatisfaction in the black community with this turn of events, but most people decided that it was better to have any blacks rather than none at all. So the boycott worked. We accomplished our aim; we caused the hiring of black salespersons where previously there had been none.

Black community reaction to all the integration efforts (in the schools, the business district, and the voter rolls) was generally supportive. Still, the predominant feeling was fear and concern. Most blacks believed that integration should have come much earlier, but many were worried about a flare-up of racial violence. Black parents particularly worried that their children might be mistreated in school.

The black businessman was in an especially difficult position. It was no secret that several blacks who had businesses in the downtown area opposed the boycott. Most of their trade came from whites, and they were afraid they might be ruined economically. To their credit, they did nothing to try to curtail the boycott, although they did a lot of talking in opposition to it.

Until 1966, Uncle Rob Wier owned a barbershop on Main Street which served an exclusively white clientele. He had long been a black leader in Starkville, but he never became publicly involved in any integration efforts. He was too concerned about economic repercussions. Yet he was always supportive. I remember him saying: "This is what must be done. I'm not actively a part of it, but my sympathies are with you. If I publicly endorse what you're doing, I'll be closed tomorrow. I'll support you silently."

The dilemma of black businessmen like Uncle Rob is too often ignored when people talk about the integration effort. Black businessmen had a lot to lose from integration, and their plight indicates the economic and personal sacrifices all blacks had to make in order to achieve the basic human rights due them as citizens of this country.

In general, the human rights revolution of the 1960s took a heavy toll from all those who participated in it.

Martin Luther King, whom I consider the most significant human rights figure of the era, gave his life for the cause. So too did Medgar Evers and the three civil rights workers who died in Neshoba County during Freedom Summer. Fannie Lou Hamer suffered for her activities, as did so many lesser known people who died, were beaten, lost their jobs, or suffered other kinds of indignities because they wanted to bring about an end to segregation.

Aaron Henry is a man who paid and who continues to pay a heavy price for his human rights activities. Of all those I can think of who have labored for black rights in Mississippi, Aaron is without doubt the most significant. He has spent his whole life working for freedom and the elimination of segregation, and in 1985 he continues his untiring efforts. During the worst days of the movement in Mississippi he had his house firebombed. Less dramatically, he has made a heavy personal sacrifice for his activities. He is a pharmacist by profession, but his human rights activities have never allowed him to concentrate on his business. He has made the sacrifice and continues to make it, and Mississippi is the better for it.

There have been others, of course, too numerous to name, who, I believe, were also instrumental in bringing about better days. In addition to hosts of nameless individuals, there were presidents, governors of Mississippi, and members of Congress from this state. In their own way, each participated in the revolution that swept across the state and nation. Some encouraged progress; others tried to slow it down. Each played some kind of role, however, because the movement swept them along as it swept everyone else during those years.

Of the presidents of the United States during the human rights years from Eisenhower to Reagan, I most admired John F. Kennedy. I was attracted to his style. He was such a welcome change from the typical old-style politician. He gave us a vision of better things to come. He proposed civil rights legislation of a kind undreamed of just a few years previously. In all honesty, however, I must say that the president who did more than any other for civil rights was Lyndon B. Johnson. When Kennedy was assassinated and Johnson took office, my initial reaction was: "Oh my goodness, here comes this Texan who's going to take us back to where we used to be." But I was wrong. From his first day in office, Johnson worked hard for freedom and equality. In the end, he did more to help American blacks than any other president in history. Kennedy proposed things, but Johnson had the know-how to get them through Congress.

The worst president for blacks was Richard Nixon, followed closely by Ronald Reagan. I believe that the thrust of both these presidencies was and is an attempt to turn back from civil rights gains. Attitudes like holding the line, not going too fast too soon, give permission for Americans to oppose further racial progress.

Over the years I have come to agree with the ideas that Frederick Douglass and W. E. B. DuBois espoused a long time ago: there can be no compromise with discrimination. The only way to fight it is to confront it constantly. The only way blacks will ever achieve full equality is by constantly facing discrimination head-on. If someone or some group is doing something I do not like and if I never say anything about it, then that person or that group assumes I am satisfied. If, on the other hand, I continually indicate my dissatisfaction, then that person or group has no excuse for continuing that action. Any compromise with discrimination only means more discrimination. Any stand against it, even if it fails, at least provides a platform for further, perhaps more successful, action.

As blacks we need to understand that our unflinching refusal to accept nothing less than equality is crucial. We have to respect ourselves if we want others to respect us. I think Muhammad Ali, in his own way, was one person who helped pave the way for this kind of thinking. Ali may be considered a clown and a show-off, but actually he says what blacks need to hear: that as a black person he is important. More blacks need to believe, if not "I am the greatest," then at least "I am somebody." More blacks have to be willing to speak out and take action against any situation or individual that tries to tell blacks, "You are nobody."

We have made progress over the past several years, but I have no illusions that the battle is over. It is not. There is still much more to be done in Starkville, in Mississippi, and in the nation. I hope, in my small way, to continue in the future to confront discrimination wherever I see it.

EPILOGUE

In 1985 I will be sixty-five, the traditional age for Americans to go into retirement. When a person reaches that age, American society tells him or her to take it easy and enjoy the fruits of long years of labor. But it is also the time in a person's life when he or she can reassess successes or failures, achievements and neglects.

Facing this milestone, I am luckier than most. My decision to tell the story of my life while I am still working at my profession has given me the opportunity to study my past without the nostalgia or the panic of retirement staring me in the face. I do not intend to retire. I cannot see myself living life any differently than I am living it now.

In assessing my life, I believe the major force in determining its direction was my childhood in Hattiesburg, Mississippi. I often think of my humble beginnings and the hardships my family and I faced—the personal hardship of divorce and the public hardship of discrimination. Thoughts of my childhood have served, all my life, to goad me, to stimulate me to try to reach the light. I recall the despair of those around me and my own inner protest. I remember thinking that there had to be something I could do to improve things. I knew deep inside that those around me were not right: my black skin was not a valid excuse for anyone holding me back—or, for that matter, for holding myself back.

173

My college years at Alcorn, my experiences in the North and in the army showed me I was right. Blacks were not by nature inferior. Discrimination, indeed, was unnecessary and wrong. Consequently, I have rebelled against anyone or anything that insisted that blackness was justification for inequality. I have tried to instill in my children and anyone who would listen that blacks are great, that we are somebody, that we can do anything we want if we simply try. Sure, I tell others, your black skin may cause some stumbling blocks, but that should only be an incentive. Discrimination should be used as a stimulus to work harder to make sure you get what you want out of life.

My life as a physician, Democratic politican, and advocate of human rights can be summarized in a few words, I think. In whatever way I could, I have tried to help open up the American system so that all people will accept others for what they are and not for their skin color. I have tried all my life to treat whites, blacks, Orientals, whatever, the same way. I have tried to see them as individuals worthy of respect simply because they are human beings made by the same God.

If I have made any kind of contribution in my life, I believe it has mainly been a passive one, despite my active participation in society. My greatest contribution has been one of example—my attempt to live my life as an example to others, particularly to other blacks. I hope that people look at me and say to themselves: "It can be done. You can be successful as a black." I hope they see me and reject society's insistence that blacks are incapable of success. I particularly hope that black youngsters see my small accomplishments and are encouraged to try to make the most of themselves.

Again, a childhood experience is my major guide. The example of Dr. Charles Smith in Hattiesburg was crucial in my development, even though he never knew it. I hope there is some black child somewhere who watches me from a distance or reads about me in the newspaper or even in this book, and receives similar inspiration.

I want those black youngsters who read these words to understand that, when I was young, I had to battle with myself not to hate white people. As I matured, however, I came to see that such an attitude was wrong. All whites are not racists. Over the years, for example, some Starkville whites helped in the boycott and in school integration and in other areas of the black struggle for equality. These are good people, the kind we must work with for the betterment of society for us all. Hate does nothing but create more hate, and the world certainly does not need more of that. What it needs is more blacks and whites working together for our common good.

As I finish this account of my life I do it in the hope that someone might receive some benefit from reading it. But I must insist that my life will not end where my narration leaves off. I intend to follow the advice I gave an October 1981 dinner meeting of our local NAACP. I said at that time: "We ought to learn to always be in the forefront of standing up for our rights. We should continue to fight with every fiber in our bodies—in a firm, nonviolent way all our lives."

INDEX

Aberdeen, MS., 151, 164
Abortion, 97–98
Academy, Starkville, 153, 155–57
AffirmativeAction Committee, MS.
   Democratic Party, 110
Alabama, 147
Alabama, University of, Family
   Practice Center, 147
Alabaster, AL., 148
Alcoholism, 10, 99
Alcorn State University (Alcorn A
   and M College), 19–34, 41, 42, 49,
   50, 56, 63, 66, 99, 144, 174
Aldermen, Starkville Board of, 133,
   134, 162
Aldridge Quarters, Hattiesburg, 11
Ali, Muhammad, 172
American Legion, 137
American Medical Association, 91–
   92
Amos and Andy, 19
Army, U.S., 29, 41, 42–57, 147, 174
Atomic Bomb, 54
Automobile factory, General Mo-
   tors, 34, 35, 38–39, 41

Band, Alcorn Marching, 26
Bank of North Mississippi, The, 139
Bankhead School, Noxubee County,
   84
Baptist Church: Second Starkville,
   83, 97, 137; in Detroit, 40; East
   Jerusalem, Hattiesburg, 8, 9
Barnett, Ross, 124
Barry, Ferdinand, 104
Basie, Count, 27
Beer Referendum, 137
Bell, William H., 26
Bell, Mrs. William H., 26
Bilbo, Theodore, 13

Birmingham, AL., 86, 148
Birth Control, 98
Black Caucus, Oktibbeha County,
   158, 161
Block Grant Committee, MS., 139
Borden Milk Company, 74
Bowles Hall, Alcorn, 22
Boycott, Starkville, 160–69
Brooks, Thomas, 158, 167
Brown v. Board of Education, 149, 154
Butler, Bennie, 127, 158, 167

Camp Barclay, TX., 43–45, 48, 49,
   50
Camp Shelby, MS., 42, 57
Carmichael, Gil, 119
Carter, Hodding III, 108
Carter, Jimmy, 115, 122–23
Carthan, Eddie, 125
Chamber of Commce, 138, 159
Chicago, 24, 37, 57–58, 59, 67, 85,
   143
Chicago *Defender,* 19, 30, 37, 39
Choctaw Indian, 2
Christmas, Frank, 27, 29
Churches: see Baptist, Holiness,
   Methodist, Oakland Chapel
Circuit Clerk, Oktibbeha County,
   127
Citizens Realty Inc., Starkville, 156
Civil Rights Act of 1964, 148
Civil Rights Division, Justice Dept.,
   155
Clark, Miss, 17
Clark, Robert, 125–26
Clarksdale, MS., 109
Clayton, Lloyd, 48
Clothes, 13, 21, 24–25, 37, 41
Cobb, W. Montegue, M.D., 60–61
Columbus, MS., 78, 106, 120, 160

177

INDEX

Colvard, D.W., 143, 145
Conferences, 1978, 1982 Democratic National, 112, 119–20
Congress, U.S., 170, 171
Congress of Industrial Organizations (CIO), 39
Congressional District: Second MS., 111; Third MS., 111
Connecticut, 34–37, 39, 41
Conner, Corinne (sister), 3, 10, 11
Conner, Douglas, M.D.: birth of, 1; genealogy of, 1–3; childhood of, 3–19; role model of: see Smith, Charles, M.D.; and segregation, 11–19, 21, 27–29, 39–40, 43–45, 51, 56, 64, 75–76, 82, 90, 91, 103, 102–05; early hatred for whites, 14; attends Alcorn A and M College, 20–37; in World War II, 29, 42–56; and wife: see Conner, Juanita Macon; views on black college education, 32–34; on Connecticut tobacco farm, 34–37; in Detroit, 37–41; in Army, 42–56; at Camp Barclay, TX., 43–45, 48–49, 50; at Walter Reed Army Hospital, 45–48; marriage of, 49–50; on troop ship, 50–52; on Okinawa, 52–56; in Chicago, 57–58; Howard University Medical School student, 59–67; internship in St. Louis, 66–71; medical practice of, 72–91; and family: see Conner listings and Holmes, Richard; and medical organizations, 91–92; and federal aid to medicine, 92–94; and physicians' fees, 94–95; and malpractice, 95–96; and medical training, 97; and religious beliefs, 97; and abortion, 97–98; and euthanasia, 98; and health maintenance, 98–101; and NAACP: see National Association for the Advancement of Colored People; political participation of, 106–41; in White House, 121–24; and civic activity, 137–39; and integration of Mississippi State University, 142–48; and Starkville Public School integration, 149–55;

and local academy, 155–57; and economic boycott, 158–69; and evaluation of civil rights revolution, 169–72
Conner, Earnest (brother), 3, 10, 11
Conner, Eileen Yvette (daughter), 84, 85, 86, 144
Conner, Elijah (grandfather), 1
Conner, Jerry (father), 1–5, 10, 11, 14, 49, 56, 57, 67
Conner, Juanita Macon (wife), 30–31, 49–50, 56–85 passim, 144, 145, 154–55
Conner, Maggie (grandmother), 1–2, 11
Conner, Mary Elnora Washington (mother), 1–19 passim, 21, 32, 35, 49, 56, 57
Conner, Sadye Yvonne, M.D. (daughter), 69–70, 72, 84, 85–86, 144, 163, 164
Conner, William (brother), 3, 10
Constitution, MS., 104
Conventions, Democratic National: 1948, 65; 1964, 107; 1968, 108; 1972, 112, 115, 119–20; 1976, 112, 115, 119–20; 1980, 112, 115, 119–20; 1984, 112, 115, 119–20; description of, 113–115
Cotton-Reader, R. B., 160–62, 163, 167
Counseling Center, Starkville Community, 75
Court, U.S. District, Aberdeen: and voter registration, 127; and school integration, 151–53, 155; and boycott, 164–66
Crumby, Booker T., M.D., 59–60

Data Processing, 65, 66
Daugherty, Richard, D.D.S., 24, 25
Davis, Benjamin O., 30
Death, determination of, 98
Delegates, National Democratic Convention, 112–15
Delta, The, 132
Democratic Party: Freedom Democratic, 107, 108; Miss. Loyalist, 107–10, 112, 113, 115; Miss. Regu-

178

lar, 107, 108, 109, 110; merger of Regulars and Loyalists, 109–11; Oktibbeha County, 116; state and national, 107–20, 124, 126, 127, 174
Depot, Hattiesburg Railroad, 4, 13
Depression, The Great, 13
Derian, Pat, 108, 120
Detroit, 35, 37–41, 42, 49, 50
Divorce of parents, 10, 11
Dixiecrats, 65
Dodd, Charles, M.D., 74
Douglass, Frederick, 15, 171
Draft, Military, 29, 41, 42
Drugs: hard, 99, 100; prescription, 100
DuBois, W.E.B., 15, 171

East Jerusalem Section, Hattiesburg, 7, 8, 9
Eastland, James, 124
Eckford, John Feddy, M.D., 74, 75, 90
Education, Black: good influence of, · 32–34
Education, Miss. State Advisory Committee to the Cabinet Committee on, 120–22
Education, U.S. Office of, 150, 151
Eisenhower, Dwight D., 170
Election Officials, Federal, 135–36
Ellington, Duke, 27
Ellis, Tyrone, 133
Emancipation Day, 9
Eureka High School, Hattiesburg, 11, 17, 18, 19, 20
Euthanasia, 97, 98
Evans, George, 73, 104
Evers, Charles, 105, 148
Evers, Medgar, 105–06, 170

Fair Employment Practices Commission (FEPC), 29
Farish St., Jackson, 50
Fees, Physicians,' 94–95
Felix Long Hospital, 75, 76, 77
Ferraro, Geraldine, 116, 117
First Amendment, 165
Florida, 115

Food, 2, 5, 6, 79, 99
Fort Sheridan, Illinois, 42, 43
Freedmen's Hospital, Washington, 59, 62–63, 67, 75
Freedom Democratic Party, 107, 108
Freedom Summer, 106, 170

Gallinger Hospital, Washington, 63, 65
Games, childhood, 7
Gandy, Fred, 73, 76, 80
Garvey, Marcus, 15
Georgia Avenue, Washington, 59, 64
Germany, 29, 51, 54
G.I. Bill, 43, 59
Goldmine, Miss, 1
Greater Alcorn Herald, 26
Grenada, MS., 160
Greyhound Bus, 21
God, 97, 174
Golden Triangle Region, MS., 120, 138

Haimes, Terry, 110
Hall, Tommy, 7
Hamer, Fannie Lou, 107, 170
Harlem Hospital, New York, 67
Harris, Fred, 112
Hart, Gary, 118
Hartford CT., 35, 36, 37
Hattiesburg, MS., 1–19 passim, 21, 28, 35, 40, 42, 57, 70, 73, 86, 101, 102, 173, 174
Health Insurance, National, 93–94
Health Services Agency, Golden Triangle, 138
Hearst, Mr., 25
Henderson Jr. High School, Starkville, 102, 165
Henry Aaron, 107, 108, 109, 148, 170
Henry, Miss, 17
High's Dairy, Washington, 65
Highway Program, Federal, 132
Highways: Sixty one, 21; Eighty Two, 132
Hinds County, 2, 50
Hippocratic Oath, 98
Hispanics, 119
History, Afro-American, 15, 97

Meharry Medical College, 37, 48, 53, 86

Memphis, 84

Meredith, James, 106, 144, 145

Meridian, MS., 132

Methodist Church, Griffin, Starkville, 148

Meyer, Donna, 153

Michigan State University Medical School, 86, 147

Middle Class, Black, 78

Miller, Dorrie, 56

Mississippi Hall, Acorn, 22, 23, 24, 27, 30

Mississippi Medical Association, 91

Mississippi Medical and Surgical Association, 91

Mississippi State University (Mississippi A and M College): segregation at, 104–05; integration of, 142–48, 150; mentioned 33, 73, 74, 131, 137, 143, 153

Mississippi, University of (Ole Miss), 33, 106, 143, 144, 145, 147, 149

Mobley, Roxie, 77

Mondale, Walter, 116, 117

Morris, Reuben, M.D., 24

Movies, 12, 40, 64, 89, 102

Murdock, Mrs., 25, 31

Naha, Okinawa, 52

Nashville, 37, 86

National Association for the Advancement of Colored People (NAACP), 102, 105, 106, 108, 130, 136, 148–49, 155, 158. 174

National Collegiate Athletic Association (NCAA), 143

National Medical Association, 85, 91, 92

Nazi racism, 29

Neshoba County, MS., 84, 170

New Jersey, 60

Newman Lumber Company, Hattiesburg, 1, 3, 4

Newman's Quarters, Hattiesburg, 1–9 passim

New York, 67, 85

Newspapers, 77, 130, 133, 153, 162

Nickens, Oswald, M.D., 48

Nicks, Rufus, 84

Nixon, Richard M., 120, 122, 123, 171

North Mississippi Medical, Dental, and Pharmaceutical Association, 91, 108

Noxubee County, 81, 84, 133

Oakland Chapel, Alcorn, 22, 23, 25, 26

Obesity, 99

Okinawa, 49, 52–55, 72

Oklahoma, 112

Okolona, MS., 76

Oktibbeha County, MS., 74, 104, 106, 127, 128–29, 133, 134, 148, 149, 150, 158, 161, 163

Oktibbeha County Training School, 50, 59, 102

Oktibbeha Educational Foundation, 156

Olympics, 1936, 29

Orchestra, Alcorn College, 27, 29

Owens, Jesse, 29

Pacific Ocean, 50–51

Pascagoula, MS., 24

Patients, 79–83, 87, 93, 96–97, 105, 164

Patterson, Tom and Lillian, 11, 21, 27, 32, 37

Pearl Harbor, 51, 56

Peters, Fenton, 154

Picayune, MS., 3, 11, 32

Pittsburgh *Courier,* 19, 30, 39

Police, 44, 104, 161, 162, 163, 166

Polish farm workers, 36–37

Politics: importance of, 139–41. See also: Conferences, Conventions, Democratic Party, Registration, Voting, White House

Poll Tax, 104

Poor People, 117–18

Professionals, Black, 78–79

Provident Hospital, Chicago, 67

Quartermaster Battalion, 31st, 48, 52

Race: in political leaflets, 130–31. See also: Education, Integration,

INDEX

NAACP, Polish Farm Workers, and Segregation
Radio, 19, 130
Randolph, A. Philip, 29
Reader's Digest, 40
Reading, 17, 40
Reagan, Ronald, 116, 117, 118, 124, 126, 170, 171
Red Cross, 54
Redmond, S. R., 31
Registrars, Federal, 106
Registration, Voting, 104, 106, 127–28, 130, 148
Republican Party, 117, 118, 119, 124, 125
Rex Theatre, Starkville, 103
Riddell, Tom, 109
Riot of 1943, Detroit, 40
Robinson, B. L., 73, 104
Robinson, W. B., 158
Roosevelt, Franklin, 13, 29, 51–52, 65
Rust College, 20

Sacramento, CA., 60
St. Louis, 37, 67–76 passim
San Francisco, 56
Scales, Hunter, M.D., 74–75, 80–81
Scholarship, Miss. Medical, 59
Schools: Bankhead, Noxubee County, 84; East Jerusalem Elementary, Hattiesburg, 7, 8; Eureka High, Hattiesburg, 11, 17, 18, 19, 20; Henderson Jr. High, Starkville, 102, 165; Oktibbeha County Training, Starkville, 50, 59, 102; Starkville Public, 142, 150–57
Seattle, 49, 50
Segregation: in Hattiesburg, 11–19, 21; at University of Southern Mississippi, 21; at Alcorn A and M College, 27–29; in Detroit, 39–40; in Army, 29, 43–45, 51, 56; in Washington, 64; in St. Louis, 70; in medicine, 75–76, 82, 90, 91, 103; in Starkville, 102–105; at Mississippi A and M College, 104–105
Senate, Miss., 129, 131–32, 133, 134
Shriver, Sargent, 120

Shubuta, MS., 1, 2
Shuqualak, MS., 81
Sickle Cell Anemia, 66
Smith, Charles, M.D., 15–16, 31, 86, 174, 175
Smith, Frank, 124
Smith, Luther, M.D., 31
Smith, Orma, 152–53, 165, 166
Smoking, 99, 100
Southeastern Athletic Conference, 143
Southern Christian Leadership Conference, 150
Southern Mississippi, University of, 21, 33
Sports, 26–27, 104, 137, 143
Stark Hotel, Starkville, 163
Starkville, MS., 50, 57, 59, 63, 64, 70–84, 102–05, 120, 127–40, 142, 147, 148, 150–69, 175
Steel Mill, Carnegie, Chicago, 57
Stennis, John C., 124, 125, 126
Strange, Dempsey, M.D. 88, 90
Stringer, E. J., D.D.S., 106
Stress, 100–01
Supreme Court, U.S., 149, 154
Surgical Technician, Army, 45–48

Taylor, Clarence, 104, 158
Technology, Medical, 89
Tennessee, 132
Television, 89, 106, 114, 115, 130, 137, 147
Texas, 144
Thomas, Rev. Riley, 8
Tobacco Farm, Connecticut, 34, 35–37
Toledo, Ohio, 148
Tougaloo College, 20, 28
Trent, Arthur, M.D., 60
Truman, Harry, 52, 65
Tuscaloosa, AL., 147

Union, 39
United States District Court, Aberdeen: see Court, U.S. District, Aberdeen

Venereal Disease, 79
Veterans Administration, 65

INDEX

Vitamins, 99
Voting, 13–14, 29, 104, 127–130, 133–36. See also: Justice Dept., Poll Tax, Registration, Voting Rights Act of 1965
Voting Rights Act of 1965, 106, 124, 127, 128, 136, 148

Wall St., New York, 118
Wallace, George, 110, 115
Walter Reed Army Hospital, 45–49, 59
Washington, Booker T., 15
Washington, D.C., 37, 45, 47–48, 58, 64, 150
Washington, March on, 29
Washington, Ras, 2
Watkins, Wes, 108
Welfare, 118

West Point, MS., 78, 120, 160, 164
West Side Park, Starkville, 163–64
Whissington, Professor, 17
White House, 47, 51, 102, 120–24
Wier, Robert, 11, 72, 73, 76, 77, 83, 84, 104, 169
Wier, Sadye H., 50, 64, 69, 72, 73, 76, 77, 83, 84
Wiley College, 144, 147
Williams, John Bell, 124
Wilson, Charles, 25, 28
Windsor, CT., 35
Winter, William, 110, 124, 125
World War II, 29, 42–56
Wright, Lucretta, 26

Young, Moses Wharton, M.D., 62

Zuber, Thomas L., M.D., 78